INTERNET SECURITY MADE EASY

RICHARD N. WILLIAMS

FLAME TREE
PUBLISHING

CONTENTS

The World Wide Web has come a long way since its origins in the 1980s. What started out as a tool for academics and researchers has morphed into the most revolutionary communication tool ever developed. In this chapter, we explore the history of the World Wide Web, how the Internet works and how security threats take advantage of inherent weaknesses in it. We also provide you with some basic advice on keeping secure when you are online.

Now that you know a little about how the World Wide Web works, it is time to explore some of the specific risks of using the Internet. In this chapter, we explore the different types of online threat, from the various kinds of malware and the consequences of infection, to identifying fraudsters and hackers. We also explain what makes you vulnerable and how you can go about ensuring that you do not fall victim.

Many of us now live some of our lives online. Whether we are on social media, chatting to friends, or logging into our online bank, we need to ensure that we are keeping our personal information safe and secure. In this chapter, we explore the various privacy and security settings employed by websites. We also explore the risks faced by young people using the Internet and what you can do to keep them safe.

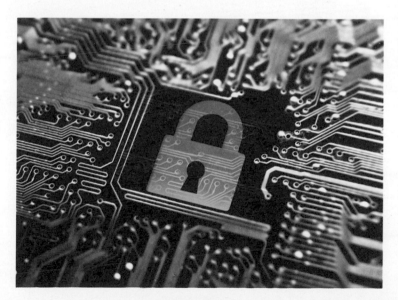

If you do not have any antivirus protection, it is time to install some. This chapter explains the importance of antivirus software, the different solutions available, how to use antivirus software to remove threats and prevent infections. We also explain what firewalls are and how they can be used to provide security, and look at some of the other software protection available.

Now that you have secured your desktop PC, it is time to look at all those other devices you use to access the Internet. Smartphones, tablet computers and laptops all come with specific online security threats, and we will show you how to secure your data, how to keep safe when accessing the Internet in public areas, as well as exploring some of the antivirus and security solutions aimed at mobile devices.

ADVANCED TROUBLESHOOTING 210

Whether you have been infected by a stubborn computer virus that you cannot remove, or your Internet browser keeps showing you unwanted adverts, we explain how you can get rid of some specific threats, recover lost data and get your computer back to good working order following an attack. We also explore the different types of hardware solutions that can help secure your network, prevent unauthorized access and add an extra level of Internet security.

INTRODUCTION

The Internet has changed our lives forever, but this communications revolution is not without its problems. As in ordinary life, there are viruses, hackers and identity fraudsters. This book is designed to help you safely navigate the online world and keep you secure from online threats.

Above: Websites such as Facebook allow us to socialize but they also contain all sorts of personal information about us.

Above: Many of us now do our banking online. The last thing we would want is for somebody to be able to access our accounts.

INTERNET SECURITY

Keeping safe online is important. As well as benefits, the Internet contains potentially harmful threats, from viruses and malware that can infect our computers, erasing our data or spying on our online activities, to hackers and ID fraudsters who want to gain access to our data for their own aims. Knowing how to defend yourself from these threats is increasingly crucial for keeping your network, computers, online accounts and family safe.

The Importance of Protection

The Internet has become a vital tool for many of us, enabling us to socialize on social media, communicate by email, shop and do our banking online. Because of this reliance on the online world, keeping secure is vital to prevent unauthorized access to our online accounts and ensure our personal information does not fall into the wrong hands.

ONLINE THREATS

When most people think of Internet security, they think of viruses, but there are many types of viruses and much more to protecting yourself online than keeping malicious software at bay. Your web presence can give hackers and fraudsters a wealth of information about you. They can even access your finances and take over your identity. Furthermore, if you have children who are using social networks and communicating with people over the World Wide Web, you want to be assured that they are doing it safely.

The Mobile Age

The Internet used to be something that you could only access on a desktop PC through a phone line. However, these days you can access the web almost anywhere. Smartphones, tablet computers, wireless access and other technologies means the World Wide Web is available everywhere, but so are online threats, and Internet security is just as important when you are using a smartphone as it is when you are using a desktop PC.

Above: We can access the Internet almost anywhere, making Internet security just as crucial for mobile devices.

USING THIS BOOK

This book has been designed to give you all the information you need to keep safe when you surf the Internet. Whether you use the Internet for socializing, to do your banking, or to download games and software, this book will help you navigate the world of Internet security and ensure you and your family can go online safely and securely.

Hot Tip

Throughout this book, we have inserted a number of hot tips and fact boxes. These are designed to help you find some simple yet effective advice on different aspects of Internet security.

Help For All

You can read this book from cover to cover, or you can use it as a reference and turn to it whenever you need help with a different aspect of online security. We have tried to cover all aspects of web protection and Internet security, from keeping viruses and malware at bay

Above: This book will help you keep your children safe when they are online.

to helping guard against hackers and ID fraudsters, as well as how to secure your Internet connection at home and ensure your children are using the Internet in safety.

Beginners to Advanced

This book is aimed at both those new to the Internet and Internet security and those with more online experience. We provide basic help on protecting your computers and online accounts, as well as some more advanced Internet security advice, such as how to manually remove viruses and malware, repair your system following an attack, or how to surf the Internet anonymously.

Cutting through the Complexity

The world of Internet security can be a complicated one, but we have tried to simplify as many aspects as we can, so if you are unsure what HyperText Mark-up Language is, or what browser cookies do, we will explain everything in a language that we are sure you will understand.

Jargon

As with the rest of the Internet, the subject of online security is full of its own jargon and terminology. However, where possible, we have provided instructions and information using the simplest possible terms. We have also included a glossary of the most common Internet security terms in our Jargon Buster (see pages 248–251).

Microsoft Office Outlook

The Add-in "F-PROT Antivirus E-mail plug-in" (C:\Program Files\FRISK Software\F-PROT Antivirus for Windows\fpoutavext.dll) cannot be loaded and has been disabled by Outlook. Please contact the Add-in manufacturer for an update. If no update is available, please uninstall the Add-in.

OK

Above: Different aspects of Internet security can be complicated but we won't expect you to deal with anything like this!

Step by Step

Throughout this book, we have included step-by-step guides to steer you through some of the more technical aspects of Internet security, such as how to adjust your browser and computer settings, install antivirus software, and adjust your social media privacy so you are more secure when you use Facebook, Twitter and other networking websites.

MALWARE AND VIRUSES

One of the most common threats to your online security is malicious software, which can cause you all sorts of problems, from spying on your online activity in a bid to steal your passwords and usernames, to disabling your computer, erasing files or even using your machine to attack other computers. In this book, we explain the difference between a computer virus and a Trojan horse, what spyware and adware are, and how to protect yourself from these and other malicious software threats.

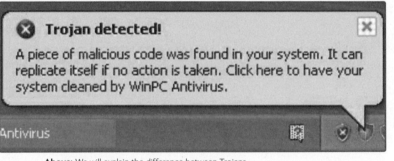

Above: We will explain the difference between Trojans and viruses and how to protect against them.

Antivirus Software

Antivirus software is one of the most crucial tools for keeping you safe online. In this book, we explain the different types of protection on offer, from free solutions that you can download and install for basic protection, to paid-for packages from some of the most respected names in Internet security software.

Hot Tip

If your computer is already infected with a virus or other malware, this book will show you how to remove the threat and secure your computer so it does not happen again.

Firewalls and Other Protection

Learning how to install a firewall is also another crucial aspect of Internet security. We not only explain what a firewall is and how it works, but we also give you step-by-step instructions on how to install and get the most out of the technology. We also provide you with some handy hints and tips on using routers and Wi-Fi access points, ensuring you are always protected no matter where you are.

HELP AND FURTHER READING

No book on Internet security can cover every conceivable aspect. Because of this, we have included helpful websites throughout and also at the end, along with useful books for those wanting more information on safe surfing.

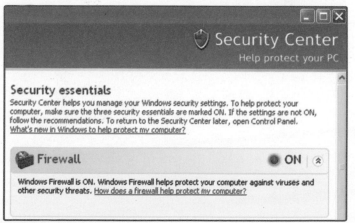

Above: Learn how to use firewalls to protect your computer and network.

WELCOME TO THE WEB

ORIGINS OF THE WWW

It is difficult to imagine the world without the Internet. Yet the Internet as we know it is just a few decades old and it is all down to just one man and his creation – the World Wide Web.

THE HISTORY OF THE WEB

The Internet has been around since the late Sixties. It grew out of a US Defense Department project called ARPANET (Advanced Research Projects Agency Network). This was a project designed to develop a secure computer communications network that could be used in the event of war (this was during the height of the Cold War) and started as a number of computer connections between various universities and research institutes.

Text-based Communication

The early Internet was great for exchanging text-based information (the first email was sent in 1971). There were no pictures, videos, search engines, or even links to other websites, just pages of text, and finding a page was extremely difficult, as you needed to know the telephone number for the computer modem where the page was based. For this reason, the only people who ever used it were academics and researchers.

Left: Early Internet usage was completely text-based.

THE FATHER OF THE WEB

The early Internet was not easy to use. Different computers used different languages, so exchanging information and making improvements to the Internet proved difficult. It took a British scientist at the European particle physics laboratory, CERN, to identify what was needed. Tim Berners-Lee came up with the idea of a standard Internet, where all users used the same language and protocols. He called it the World Wide Web.

Developments

To enable the creation of the World Wide Web, Tim Berners-Lee brought together several ideas and innovations, which included the following.

- **HTML (HyperText Markup Language):** A universal language used by all web pages to format, exchange and publish information.

- **URL (Uniform Resource Identifier):** A unique address for each website, allowing users a simple method of gaining access to a website.

- **HTTP (HyperText Transfer Protocol):** Developed in conjunction with the computer mouse, HTTP allowed web pages to be connected by use of hypertext words, now commonly called links.

Above: Tim Berners-Lee created the World Wide Web as we know it today.

Did You Know?

At the end of 1992, there were only 26 websites in existence on the World Wide Web. Today, there are over a trillion web pages on hundreds of millions of websites.

Access For All

In what has to be one of the most magnanimous gestures in history, Tim Berners-Lee and the directors at CERN issued a statement in 1993 declaring that the World Wide Web was to become freely available for everybody to use. This move saw the birth of the Internet as we know it today, which in a few short years has become arguably the most powerful communications tool ever created.

GROWTH OF THE WEB

Since the World Wide Web became freely available for everybody to use, its growth has been exponential, aided by all sorts of technologies and developments.

Above: Amazon was the first large, commercial ecommerce site. It originally sold just books, but now sells a wide range of products.

○ **Web browsers:** Programs called browsers allowed people to access websites by making HTML easier to use.

○ **Search engines:** In the mid-Nineties, the first search engines appeared, making it much easier to find and access information.

○ **Commerce:** The first ecommerce websites appeared in the mid-Nineties, which helped to change the way the world does business.

THE WEB TODAY

The World Wide Web is no longer the preserve of a few academics and researchers. Today, over 1.7 billion people around the world use the Internet. The web continues to develop. In the early days, modem connections made uploading and downloading non-text files slow and cumbersome; with today's superfast broadband, we can now use the web to access images, videos, music and other multimedia.

The Mobile Web

The way we access the web has changed dramatically too. With the advent of smartphones and tablet computers, we no longer need to be tied to a computer, which means we have access to the Internet wherever we are and whatever we are doing.

Did You Know?

Although now used interchangeably, strictly speaking, the 'Internet' is the network of computers, while the 'World Wide Web' is the term for the websites on the Internet.

Above: Mobile devices have allowed us to access the World Wide Web almost anywhere we like.

INTERNET USE

What started as an information portal for communicating text has become an integral part of our daily lives, allowing us to do a whole host of things online, and many of us are becoming increasingly dependent on the virtual world for many of our day-to-day activities.

Communication

One of the most revolutionary aspects of the Web is how it has changed the way in which we communicate. Before the web, there were primarily three ways to connect with someone – by post, over the phone, or face to face. The web has introduced a number of different methods of communication, all of which have made the world a much smaller place.

- **Email:** Email is instant and enables you to attach all sorts of files to your messages. These days, much of the world's correspondence takes place via email.

Above: Social media site Facebook has over a billion users.

- **Social media:** Websites such as Twitter, Facebook and LinkedIn have enabled people to socialize, network and build relationships online and with people from across the globe.

- **Instant messaging:** Instant messaging (IM) has enabled real-time communication between people no matter where they are in the world.

- **VoIP**: Voice-over-Internet Protocol now allows people to have global, real-time text, voice, and even face-to-face communication for little or no cost.

News and Information

The Web is now most people's primary source of news and information. Using search engines such as Google, the world's knowledge is literally at your fingertips. Websites such as Wikipedia have replaced traditional encyclopedias, while nearly all news organizations have an online presence. Furthermore, access to news is much quicker, with news stories often breaking on websites and social media forums before the mainstream news networks can broadcast them.

Above: VoIP services such as Skype let people speak to each other over the Internet.

Commerce

The commercial world is now reliant on the Internet too. All sorts of transactions that once required a trip to the high street can now be conducted online.

- **Shopping**: Online shopping has revolutionized the way we shop. Buying online is now as common as shopping on the high street, and nearly every big-name retailer has a web presence.

- **Financial Transactions**: Many people now use the web to keep abreast of their finances, whether it is checking their bank balance or paying bills.

Above: Online banking has made keeping on top of your finances much easier.

○ **Reservations:** Airline tickets, hotel rooms and restaurant bookings can be made over the Internet.

Entertainment

The web has also radically changed the way we access entertainment. Films, TV shows, music, video games and electronic books are now available to download online. You can even watch TV channels as they are broadcast or listen to live radio.

Business

Many people now rely on the Internet to make their living. Whether it is selling goods and services online, or operating as a freelance writer, designer or consultant, the web has made doing business so much easier.

Marketing

The web offers all sorts of ways to get your message across. It is now possible for those in the creative industries, such as authors, musicians and video producers, to reach their audience without the need for distributors or publishers, and advertisers can use social media to reach potential customers.

Above: Entertainment websites such as Netflix let you access films and TV shows over the Internet.

THE ATTACKS BEGIN

While the web has hugely expanded our opportunities, it has also made us vulnerable. Since the very start of the World Wide Web, users with malicious motives began to take advantage of it.

BRAVE NEW WORLD

Tim Berners-Lee's vision for the World Wide Web was a system that would bring the world closer together, enabling free access to information and the exchange of ideas. This concept meant that very little thought was given to security, and in the very early days of the web, when there were just a few users, the need to protect information and data did not arise. However, that was soon to change.

The Threat

It didn't take long before malicious users threatened the basic ideals of the web by taking advantage of the ever-increasing number of users. Computer viruses, hackers and people seeing the Web as an opportunity to commit crime have meant that security became an ever-increasing concern for Internet users.

Above: The web was designed without much thought given to Internet security.

HACKING

Gaining unauthorized access to a computer or the data that it holds is known as hacking. However, computer hacking predates both the World Wide Web and the Internet. In fact, the first hackers had nothing to do with computers at all.

The First Computer Hackers

The first hackers appeared in the 1960s and 1970s. During this time, the most rapidly developing technology was in telecommunications, and a practice developed in America where by people would try to bypass telecoms systems in an attempt to get free phone calls – a practice that became known as 'phreaking'. When computers gained popularity in the late 1970s and early 1980s, many of the people who had been involved in phreaking began to take an interest in this emerging technology and started to gain unauthorized access to computer systems, often just for the fun of it.

Above: John Thomas Draper, one of the most famous figures in the computer-hacking fraternity.

Did You Know?

Former phone phreaker and computer programmer John Thomas Draper, known as Captain Crunch, gained notoriety in the 1970s following several high-profile arrests, and is considered by many to be the father of the modern-day computer hacker.

Legislation

Until 1986, no specific law governed unlawful access to computers. However, following several high-profile hacks, the US became the first country to outlaw the practice when Congress passed the Computer, Fraud and Abuse Act.

MALWARE

People soon realized that hacking into a computer was not the only way to gain unauthorized access or cause chaos. Hackers soon discovered they could use tiny software programs to infect a computer and cause its systems to crash.

Computer Viruses

The term 'computer virus' was first coined in 1984, when computer scientist Fred Cohen wrote a paper warning of the potential of these infectious programs, which could replicate and spread through networks, just as biological viruses do in living hosts. Early viruses were usually hidden in legitimate programs and spread by removable media such as floppy disks, the precursor to CDs and memory sticks.

Left: Early computer viruses were spread by floppy disks.

However, the rise of the World Wide Web meant there was soon a much easier way to spread a computer virus from machine to machine.

ONLINE CON ARTISTS

Along with computer viruses and computer hackers, another threat soon surfaced on the World Wide Web – online fraud. When more and more people started gaining access to the Internet, it became possible for fraudsters to target thousands of people at once.

419 Scams

One of the earliest and still most common computer frauds is known as the 419 scam. This originated in Nigeria and is named after the Nigerian criminal code that deals with fraud. There are many variants of the 419 scam, but they usually involve somebody posing as a high-ranking official, such as a prince or general needing to transfer a large sum of money out of the country. The fraudster often offers an inordinately large sum of money to victims if they agree to let the fraudster use their bank account for the transfer, and once the fraudster has hold of the victim's bank details, they can plunder their account.

> | ← | Delete forever | Not spam | 📁 ▾ | 🏷 ▾ | More ▾ | ⟨ ⟩ |
>
> Be careful with this message. Similar messages have been used to steal people's personal information. Unless you trust the sender, don't click on links or reply with personal information. **Learn more**
>
> FROM THE DESK OF THE PROMOTIONS MANAGER
> POWERBALL LOTTERY E-GAMES PROMOTIONS
> UNTIED KINGDOM.
>
> RE: AWARD WINNING EMAIL NOTIFICATION!!!
>
> We wish to notify and congratulate you on the selection of your email ID as the jackpot winning entry in the Powerball E-Games Promotions, being the inaugural edition of our new e-lottery program. Your email ID identified with Ballot No. PBL7435890481 and was selected among the winning email ID's in the draws held today using the latest version of the Computer Random Selection System (CRSS) from the 50,000 promotional entries submitted by our international software support/affiliate

Above: Another variant of the 419 scam is sending an email that claims you have won a large sum of money in a lottery but you need to hand over your bank details to claim the prize.

Hot Tip

One of the golden rules when trying to identify online fraud is that if something seems too good to be true, then it most likely is. Never divulge personal details to somebody you do not know, no matter what they are offering you.

THE DEFENCES

As computer viruses, hacking and online fraud became more common, people came up with different methods to defend computers and keep data safe. Many of these systems predate the World Wide Web, but the popularity of the Internet has meant these methods to neutralize security threats took on new importance.

○ **Firewall**: Named after the fireproof barrier that protects connected properties in the event of a fire, a firewall blocks access to a system and only lets through data that adheres to specific criteria.

○ **Antivirus**: As computer viruses became more prominent, developers created programs to clean infected systems, known as antivirus software.

Above: Antivirus software such as McAfee has become a necessity for keeping out computer viruses.

○ **Encryption**: To prevent unauthorized access to data as it travels around the Internet, encryption was developed to make the data difficult to read or decode without a decryption key.

○ **Spam filters**: Used to identify unsolicited emails and those from fraudsters.

The Arms Race

Ever since hacking and computer viruses emerged, a battle has been raging between the hackers and those trying to stop them infiltrating computer systems. As the sophistication of security measures increases, so does the sophistication of the hackers attempting to break into the systems.

CYBER ATTACKS

The malicious use of computers is known as cyber crime. It can range from criminals wanting to steal an individual's personal information to State-sponsored cyber attacks, where a nation targets another country's computer systems either to steal information or cause chaos.

Cost

Because of the prevalence of cyber crime, the global Internet security industry is worth an estimated £70 billion, yet it is estimated that cyber attacks cost the global economy many times more than that.

Above: Cyber crime costs the global economy hundreds of billions of pounds.

STAYING SAFE

For the average individual, there is little to fear from State-sponsored cyber attacks, but it is still important to protect yourself from cyber crime. In the next section, we will explore the various security threats and the consequences of poor Internet security.

THE RISKS

We will explore online threats in more detail in the next chapter, but in order to understand the importance of Internet security, we will take a quick look at some of the most common threats and the dangers they pose.

INTERNET DEPENDENCE

As the World Wide Web has evolved, many of us have become ever more dependent on the virtual world. We now rely on the Internet for all sorts of things, from financial transactions and online banking, to communicating with friends and colleagues. If our computers, smartphones or tablets become compromised, the results can be catastrophic, especially if important information, such as your online bank details, fall into the wrong hands.

Protecting Yourself

Because of this dependence on the World Wide Web, Internet security is now crucial to protect us from the array of online threats that lurk in the virtual world. But before you can arm yourself, it is a good idea to know just what is out there.

Did You Know?

'Computer virus' is often used as a broad term to describe all types of malware, and most antivirus software is designed to remove not just viruses but also other malware threats.

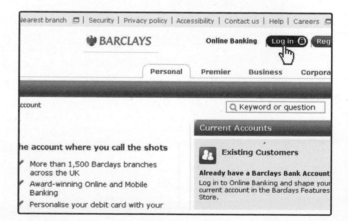

Above: To ensure safe online banking is just one of the reasons why you need Internet security.

MALWARE

Malware describes a whole gamut of malicious programs designed to compromise computers, steal data or hijack your machine. Malware is simply a contraction of **mal**icious soft**ware**. We will look at malware in more detail in the next chapter, but for now, it is worth understanding the different types that are out there.

Computer Virus

This is a form of malware that is able to replicate itself and spread from machine to machine by attaching itself to a legitimate program, which, when launched, releases the virus.

Trojan Horse

A malicious program disguised as a normal or innocent file. Once the file is opened, the Trojan is activated and can be used to gain remote access to your computer.

Above: Trojans are often sent in email attachments.

Worms

A computer virus that replicates itself over a network. Worms can spread independently, without the need for a user to open a file or run a program.

Spyware

Designed to spy on your computer, once activated, spyware can monitor your keystrokes, steal passwords and steal data from your hard drive.

Adware

Designed to bombard you with advertisements, adware normally infects an Internet browser and can assail you with annoying pop-ups – extra windows that appear on your screen – that prevent you from browsing normally.

Bot

A software program designed to do a specific task. Bots can work silently together on thousands of machines, unbeknown to the users, and attack websites and other computer systems (this connecting of bots is known as a botnet).

Ransomware

Holds a computer for ransom by seizing control and preventing normal access until the user pays to have the malware removed.

Rootkit

Malware designed to hide on a machine and be undetectable by security systems and users, often by taking advantage of vulnerabilities in software systems.

Pharming

These can change bookmarks and other files in your Internet browser and take you to a bogus or scam site.

Spam

Unsolicited messages, usually sent by email, which can clog up inboxes.

Scareware

These are usually designed to scare users into paying for an unnecessary product by claiming a virus has infected the computer.

❌ **Your computer is infected!** ✖

Windows has detected spyware infection!

It is recomended to use special antispyware tools to pervent data loss. Windows will now download and install the most up-to-date antispyware for you.

Click here to protect your computer from spyware!

Above: Scareware can pretend to be authentic messages from your operating system.

HACKING

As discussed earlier in this chapter, hacking is the unauthorized access of a computer, network or online account. Hacking is done for a multitude of reasons, some more nefarious than others.

- **Challenge**: Some hackers just enjoy the challenge of beating security systems; often these hackers will infiltrate high-profile networks.

- **Criminality**: Hackers often target machines to steal data, obtain personal information, steal money or cause disruption.

- **Ethical hacking**: A legal form of hacking, where somebody is hired to hack into a system to check system security.

> ### Hot Tip
> Even the most secure and expensive computer networks can be hacked, so there is no guaranteed way of keeping hackers out. But you can make life much more difficult for them by taking proper Internet security precautions.

Above: Hacking predates the World Wide Web and remains a huge problem.

Methods of Hacking

The problem with trying to prevent hacking is that hackers utilize a myriad of techniques to gain access to a computer system or to hack people's online accounts. These include taking advantage of system vulnerabilities, the sophisticated use of malware and 'phishing' techniques (for more information about hacking and what you can do about it, see pages 76–89.)

PHISHING

One of the simplest ways of gaining access to a computer or to someone's online account is to fool people into handing over their login details, such as a password or username. This is known as 'phishing'. One of the most common methods of phishing is to send an email that appears to come from a legitimate source, such as a bank or social media account. These emails provide a link to log in and prompt victims to do so, usually by suggesting there is a problem with their account. However, these links often take you to a fake site (known as a 'spoof' site) that looks like the real thing but is designed to get hold of login details.

IDENTITY THEFT

Because we live so much of our lives online, it can be very easy for somebody to pose as us if they have the right personal information. This is known as identity theft. Whether it is by hacking, phishing or malware, if somebody gets enough personal information about you, they can open up bank accounts, obtain credit and commit criminal offences, all in your name (we will look at identity theft in more detail on pages 67–75).

Above: A phishing email claiming to be from Twitter, prompting the account holder to log in.

OTHER THREATS

Malware, hackers and fraudsters are not the only threats posed by the online world. Proper Internet security can also help you guard against:

- **Harassment/Bullying:** Taking part in online forums or using social media can mean you can come into contact with people intent on bullying, harassing or threatening you, a practice known as 'trolling'.

- **Wireless piggybacking**: With so many Internet connections now wireless, it is possible for somebody to use your connection without you knowing it; they may even be downloading illegal files or hacking.

- **Offensive content**: There may be lost of Web content that you may not want see or want your children to see, such as pornographic or violent websites.

Above: Internet security can help keep your children safe.

CONSEQUENCES OF POOR INTERNET SECURITY

Failing to protect ourselves from online threats can result in all sorts of consequences, ranging from minor inconveniences to serious financial traumas.

○ **System failure**: Malware can cause systems to run slowly, crash and even cause permanent damage to a computer.

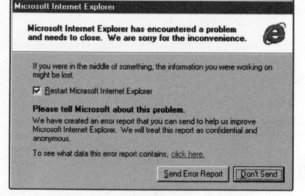

○ **Internet problems**: You may find you lose your Internet connection because of a security issue, or your connection speed may slow down, or you may be unable to access certain web pages.

○ **Data loss**: Hackers and malware may not only steal and copy your personal data and files, but they could also cause it to be permanently erased.

Above: System errors can often be a sign of malware.

○ **Financial loss**: If somebody gains access to financial websites, such as your bank account, you could lose money.

○ **Identity fraud**: If someone uses your personal information, you may become liable for loans and other financial obligations taken out under your name.

○ **Infection**: If you have poor Internet security, you may pass viruses and other malware on to friends, relatives and co-workers.

○ **Privacy**: Poor Internet security means people may be able to access your social media accounts, photos stored on your hard drive and other personal data.

AUTHENTICATING IDENTITY

The first line of defence in Internet security is the various methods employed by websites and service providers to help you prove who you are. In this section, we will look at the different ways websites can authenticate your identity.

IT'S ME, HONEST!

Before the World Wide Web, if you wanted to withdraw money from your account, pay for something using a chequebook, or access some personal information, it would normally

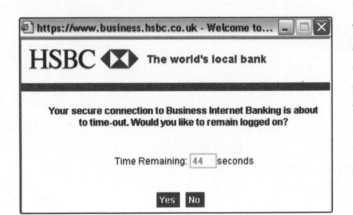

involve you handing over some type of identification, such as a driving licence or banker's card, and then providing a signature. In the online world, these methods of proving identity are not practical, so other forms of identity authentication are needed.

Left: Online banks will often log you off after a certain amount of time of inactivity.

Did You Know?

Many secure websites will time out after a set amount of time of inactivity. This is in case you have left your computer unattended and forgotten to log off. Once timed out, you have to log in again to resume using the website.

ONLINE IDENTIFICATION

There are three stages to online identification that most websites and computers commonly use in order to authenticate you are who you say are.

- **Identifier:** To begin the process of identification and help the computer or website identify you, some form of identifier is required. This is often a username or email address.

- **Authentication:** This is a system designed for you to be able to prove you are who you say you are. The most common authenticators are passwords or PIN numbers (personal identification number).

- **Authorization:** If you have successfully entered your password or PIN, the system grants authorization for you to enter the website by logging you in.

Email Validation

Many online services, such as social media sites, require you to have a valid email address before you sign up. This email address is used as part of the identification process. In order to gain access to your account, you may first have to validate that you own the email address attached to it. This is usually done by clicking a link sent in an email to the address stipulated.

Above: Many online account providers require you to verify your identity by email

Username

The most common identifier used by websites and computers is the username. Usernames have to be unique. Some websites use an email address as a username, others ask you to create one, and some will create one for you.

Passwords

Passwords are by far the most common authenticators used by websites and computers. Most passwords are six to twelve digits long and use both letters and numbers. When you enter a password, it is normally obscured, for example appearing on screen as asterisks (*), to prevent anybody looking over your shoulder and seeing it.

Hot Tip

Most websites requiring a username and password have a check box for remembering your login details. Make sure you do not tick it if you are using a public or shared computer to prevent somebody else logging in using your details.

AUTHENTICATION OVERLOAD

Because of the sheer number of websites, online accounts and social media platforms people sign up to these days, it can be nigh-on impossible to memorize every single password and username combination. For this reason, some people use the same password for all their accounts. However, this is very bad practice, because if one account is compromised, the same details can be used to hack into all the others.

Cookies

Websites store your account details in little files on your computers known as cookies. This enables a computer to add further verification that you are who you say you are, as well as allowing your Internet browser to remember your username and password for you.

HALIFAX   ▸ Mobile

Welcome to Online Banking

If you don't already use Online Banking, it's simple to **register online**.

Enter your username and password to sign in.

Username
Myaccount

Password
••••••••••••

☑ Remember my username on this computer [?]

Left: Entering a username and password to access a bank account. Note the check box to remember the details.

OTHER ONLINE SECURITY MEASURES

As well as username and passwords, websites deploy a host of other security measures to help with the authentication process.

- **Memorable information**: When you sign up to a website or service, you may be asked to provide some memorable information such as your first school or mother's maiden name.

- **IP address**: Some websites restrict you to logging in on specific computers and won't allow access if your IP (Internet Protocol) address, the unique identifier of your computer, is different to the one registered to your account.

- **PIN**: Personal Identification Numbers are often used in conjunction with passwords on secure sites.

My memorable information

Please enter characters 4, 5 and 6 from your memorable information then click the continue button.

We will never ask you to enter your FULL memorable information.

This sign in step improves your security.

Character 4   Character 5   Character 6

[d   ▼]   [Select ▼]   [Select ▼]

▸ Having problems signing in?

☒ Cancel   Continue

Above: Entering memorable information to log into a bank account.

Password Lock

Many password systems, especially on secure servers, will lock you out if you enter the incorrect password several times (usually three times). This is to stop people attempting to guess a password or to prevent software bots from running through every possible password combination to hack into a system. If you are locked out of an account, you may have to contact the administrators before you can log back in.

Hot Tip

In the next section, we will explore how to create strong passwords as well as provide you with some tips for remembering them.

CAPTCHA Codes

Another system designed to ensure a user is a human being and not a software bot is the use of CAPTCHA codes (Completely Automated Public Turing Test; a Turing test is something designed to tell the difference between people and machines). Usually, these are visuals of letters and numbers, which have to be read and correctly entered.

Type the two words:

reCAPTCHA
stop spam.
read books.

Right: Entering a CAPTCHA code.

PASSWORD ADVICE

Passwords are your virtual key for gaining access to your online accounts. However, as with other types of keys, you have to make sure they do not fall into the wrong hands, which means ensuring your passwords are secret, safe and secure.

SETTING A PASSWORD

Most websites that require you to create a password insist on at least eight letters or digits. The longer the password, the more secure it is, but the harder it is to remember.

Strong Passwords

Passwords should be strong. A strong password is one that cannot be guessed by somebody else. The strongest type of password contains letters (both upper and lower case) and numbers, and in some cases symbols (although these are not always permitted).

CREATING A STRONG PASSWORD

The problem with passwords is that you have to remember them. Random letters and numbers may

Above: Creating usernames and passwords on Twitter.

Hot Tip

Never use personal information in your usernames or passwords, such as telephone numbers or dates of birth, as this information is not only easy to guess but can also be used to compromise other online accounts.

well make a strong password but they can be difficult to remember. However, there are several methods of creating passwords that are both memorable and strong.

Replacing Letters With Numbers

1. Choose a unique word or phrase that you can use to identify the online account you are creating a password for, such as 'money place' for a bank, or 'talk land' for a social media website.

2. Replace every other letter with a number or symbol that looks similar, such as 'm@n3y p1a6e'.

3. Replace spaces with an underscore and capitalize every second letter, as in 'm@N3y_P1a6e'.

Microsoft
Safety & Security Centre

Home   Security   Privacy   Family Safety   Resources

Search Microsoft Security

Check your password—is it strong?

Your online accounts, computer files, and personal information are more secure when you use strong passwords to help protect them.

Test the strength of your passwords: Type a password into the box.

Password: ▮▮▮▮▮▮▮▮▮▮▮▮

Strength: ▮▮▮▮ ▮▮▮▮ **Strong**

Note This does not guarantee the security of the password. This is for your personal reference only.

What is a strong password?

I want to...

⊕ Help kids stay safe
⊕ Avoid scams and
⊕ Protect my inform
⊖ Create better pass

Get password guidan
Create strong passw
Reset your Microsoft password

Above: Microsoft's password checker.

Hot Tip

You can check how strong a password is by using websites such as https://www.microsoft.com/en-gb/security/pc-security/password-checker.aspx

Song Lyrics

Another method for creating memorable and strong passwords is to use a favourite line from a song.

1. Start with a memorable line from a song, such as 'She loves you yeah, yeah, yeah.'

2. Capitalize each word and remove the spaces between the words, then remove all the vowels: ShLvsYYhYhYh.

3. Replace every second or third letter with its corresponding number in the alphabet: Sh12vs25Yh25hY8.

LOOKING AFTER YOUR PASSWORD

Once you have set your password, you need to keep it safe and secure.

- **Keep it secret**: Never tell anybody your passwords. If you think that someone else knows a password, change it immediately.

- **Privacy**: When you are entering a password on a public computer, make sure nobody can see your keystrokes.

- **Do not recycle**: When creating a new password, do not use one that you have used before.

- **Storing passwords**: Avoid writing passwords down. If you have to, disguise them in sentences and never store them on your computer.

Email:

Password:

☑ Remember me

By selecting "Remember me" you will stay logged into this computer until you click logout. If this a public computer please do not use this feature.

Login   or Sign up for Facebook

Above: Uncheck the 'Remember me' box on any shared or public computers.

- **Beware**: Of email claiming to be from your account provider and asking for your password. Online account providers almost never ask for your password.

- **Public computers**: Make sure a browser on a public computer is not remembering your passwords and always log off when you have finished.

CHANGING YOUR PASSWORD

Because you never know when your details or the websites that you have frequented have been compromised, it is important to change your passwords regularly. Do this about every three months, but do not change all your online accounts at once, stagger them, just in case somebody is monitoring your computer activity.

Password Reset

If you forget your password, all is not lost. Most websites provide a password-reset facility to allow you to create a new password.

1.   On the login page, there should be a 'Forgotten your password?' or 'Reset password' link.

2.   After you click this link, you may be asked to confirm that you want to reset your password.

Hot Tip

If you think the email address that is attached to your online accounts has been compromised, change it, as anybody with access to your email could reset all your passwords and gain access to your accounts.

Above: Clicking reset password link on Twitter.

3.   Once confirmed, your account provider will send a link to your email address.

4.   Click this link to reset and create a new password.

Left: Password reset link sent to your email.

PASSWORD CHECKLIST

Because passwords are so important for protecting your online security, here is a checklist of Dos and Don'ts for keeping passwords strong and secure.

- **Do**: Use upper- and lower-case letters, numbers and keyboard symbols where possible in your passwords.

- **Do**: Make your password at least eight characters in length, longer if you can remember it.

- **Don't**: Use personal information in your passwords, such as birthdays or names of family members.

- **Don't**: Use any information somebody could guess from reading your social media pages, such as your favourite sports team or the town in which you live.

- **Don't**: Use simple or plain words, ascending or descending numbers, or keyboard patterns such as 'qwerty' in your passwords.

- **Don't**: Tell anybody your password.

- **Do**: Remember to change your password regularly.

Hot Tip

Never use a variant of the word 'password', such as 'password1' or 'pa55w0rd'. These are by far the most common passwords in use, and the easiest to crack.

Password
Change your password or recover your current one.

Associate your mobile phone with your Twitter account for enhanced security. more.

Current password

Forgot your password?

New password

Verify password

Save changes

Above: Changing a password on Twitter.

THE DANGERS

WHAT MAKES YOU VULNERABLE?

While major cyber attacks against big companies often make the headlines, you do not have to be a large organization to be vulnerable to attack. Almost anybody can become a victim, especially if you have inadequate Internet security.

TEMPTATION

The speed at which the World Wide Web has grown has been incredible. In just a couple of decades, it has gone from being a tool for a handful of researchers and academics to being ubiquitous. Millions of people now rely on the Internet for work, business and socializing. However, not everybody who uses the Internet does so with good motives. The Internet has become a tempting target for criminals or for people intent on doing harm.

Unseen Enemy

Unlike crimes committed in the real world, online criminals can commit their misdeeds anywhere in the world and from the comfort of their own home. Finding and prosecuting cyber criminals is also extremely difficult, so people who do this sort of thing believe they have little to fear.

Left: Cyber crime is an increasing problem.

Candy from a Baby

Another reason why so many people get involved in cyber crime is that it can be very easy, primarily because so many computers lack adequate Internet security, which makes them vulnerable to attack.

Continual Access

In the early days of the Internet, when somebody wanted to connect, they would plug a phone line into a modem, and when they finished, they would disconnect again. These days, most homes have high-speed, always-on connections, which can cause security issues.

○ **Constant point of entry:** An Internet connection serves as a point of entry for attack, and always-on connections mean this point of entry is always open.

○ **Static IP (Internet Protocol) address:** With dial-up modems, IP addresses changed every time you connected to the Internet, which made it harder for attackers to locate you. Modern connections have IP addresses that never change.

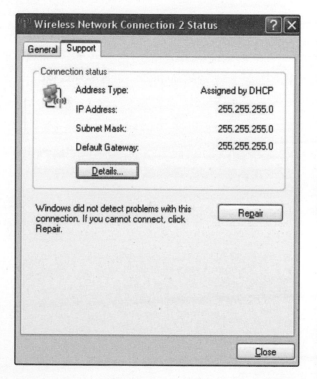

Above: IP addresses are unique numbers that can be used to identify your location.

Did You Know?

An IP address serves as a unique location identifier. They are normally a series of one to four digit numbers separated by dots, for example 1.160.10.240.

SYSTEM VULNERABILITY

Computer systems and software are always advancing in complexity. As software developers strive to add new features to their products, operating systems and programs become increasingly complex, and this complexity makes it difficult to identify weak points and vulnerabilities. While software developers try to identify problems before they release the product, quite often software contains inherent flaws when it hits the market, which hackers can take advantage of.

Operating Systems

The main program used by your computer to manage your hardware and software is known as the operating system (OS). Flaws in operating systems are particularly common, primarily because they are such large programs and have to do so many different tasks. OS developers constantly release updates to fix problems. However, by the time the update is released, malicious programs or hackers may have already exploited these flaws.

Above: Microsoft's Windows series is the most common operating system for PCs, but others include Linux, OS X for Macs, and iOS and Android for smartphones and tablets.

Internet Browsers

Web browsers, such as Internet Explorer, Chrome and Safari, are the main applications used to interact with the World Wide Web.

Did You Know?

When software and operating system manufacturers identify vulnerabilities, they often release a fix known as a patch that you can download to 'patch up' the problem.

As such, web browsers are exposed to more malicious content than other programs on our computers. Malicious websites and malware often exploit weaknesses in web browsers as a means of attack. As with operating systems, browsers require regular updates to fix these vulnerabilities.

Other Software

Web browsers and operating systems are not the only software to contain vulnerabilities that can be exploited by attackers. These days, all sorts of programs require access to the Internet, from games to office programs, and if there are flaws in these applications, it can be a way in for a malicious user.

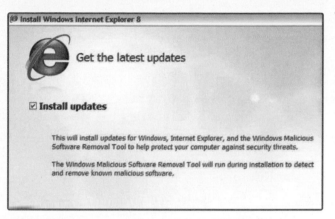

Above: Make sure you set your Internet browser to install updates.

HARDWARE VULNERABILITIES

Software is not the only aspect of our computers that can contain vulnerabilities; much of the hardware we use to connect to the Internet can also be flawed or improperly installed, leaving us open to attack.

Routers

A router is the device that lets you connect to the Internet. Its main function is to forward Internet data to and from our computers. In this respect, it acts as a gateway, so any vulnerability in a router can result in an easy way in for attackers. These days, most people use wireless routers, which have the added risk of people being able to exploit the Wi-Fi signal to access our systems.

Hot Tip

If you use a wireless router, make sure you use a password for connecting to it, otherwise anybody could gain access to your Internet connection.

Above: A secure Wi-Fi connection requires a password for access.

FIREWALLS

Firewalls are either software or hardware gateways that act as barriers, blocking data coming from the Internet unless it adheres to certain rules or criteria. Not having a firewall installed can result in your Internet connection being an open door for any hacker or malicious software to enter your system.

INSTALLING SOFTWARE FIREWALLS

Some of the most common operating systems come with a firewall built in. We will discuss how to use firewalls in more detail on pages 165–68, but in the meantime, if you want to know how to activate your firewall, just follow these steps.

Windows
1. Click **Start** and select **Control Panel**.

2. In **Windows XP** select **Security Center**, in **Windows 7** or **8** select **System and Security**.

3. In **Windows XP** check the round red button next to **Firewall** so it goes green. In **Windows 7** or **8**, click the link that says **Turn Firewall on or off** and check the button that says **Turn on Windows Firewall**.

Mac OS X
1. Click the Apple symbol (top left) and select **System Preferences** in the pull-down menu.

2. Select **Security** or **Security & Privacy**.

Above: In Windows, the firewall settings are contained in the control panel settings for System and Security.

Above: Turning the firewall on in Windows.

Above: In Mac OS X, select Security & Privacy in System Preferences.

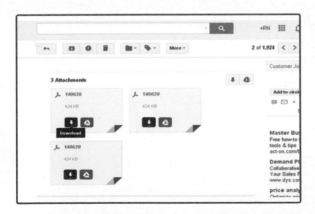

Above: Turning the firewall on in OS X.

Did You Know?

Due to the way smartphones and tablets connect to the Internet, there is little need for firewalls on these devices, although some firewall and security apps have been developed. (For more information *see* pages 205–06.)

Above: Email attachments can be a source of malware.

3. Click the Firewall tab. You may have to unlock the pane by clicking the lock in the lower-left corner and entering an administrator username and password.

4. Click **Turn on Firewall** or **Start** to activate the firewall.

HUMAN VULNERABILITY

Hardware and software vulnerabilities are not the only weak links in the Internet security chain. Quite often, users are responsible for letting in threats such as viruses or hackers. For instance, opening email attachments from people you do not know is one of the most common ways viruses get onto machines.

Education

While most people have concerns about Internet security and are aware of threats such as viruses, few people keep themselves up to date with the different ways to protect a computer system from attack. This is partly due to the rapid rate at which Internet technology advances, and secondly, users often install some form of security, such as antivirus software, and think that it will offer them 100 per cent protection, which is rarely the case. Internet security requires a holistic approach, with good practices running in tandem with hardware and software solutions.

Common Bad Practices

Computer users are often guilty of some common computer bad practices that make them more vulnerable to attack.

- **No protection:** Having no Internet security systems in place, such as antivirus software and firewalls, can almost guarantee your computer will suffer from an attack at some point.

- **Passwords:** Weak passwords, using the same password for all accounts, or divulging your passwords to other people are also common reasons why people suffer an online attack.

- **File sharing:** While peer-to-peer file sharing is a useful way to swap files with people you know, files from unknown sources can sometimes contain viruses.

Above: Files from file-sharing websites, such as ISOHunt, can sometimes contain viruses.

- **Attachments:** Opening attachments from people you do not know, or not having some antivirus software to scan them, can unleash malware.

- **Personal details:** Giving out too much personal information on social media websites can lead to people guessing passwords or knowing enough to assume your identity (identity fraud).

- **Out-of-date software:** Running old software or not updating operating systems, programs and antivirus software can make a computer vulnerable.

KEEPING SECURE

Because of the number of vulnerabilities that threaten our Internet security, the first step to staying protected is to fix as many of them as possible.

○ **Connection:** Make sure your Wi-Fi connection is secured by a password to stop people piggybacking on it.

○ **Firewall:** Install a software firewall on your computer or laptop. If your operating system does not include one, consider buying one. (For more information about firewalls, see pages 165–68.)

Above: Firewalls, software updates and antivirus protection are all crucial for Internet security.

○ **Antivirus:** Make sure you have some form of antivirus software installed. (See pages136–64 for more details about the different solutions available.)

○ **Update:** Keep your operating system, Internet browser and programs regularly updated to fix any vulnerabilities.

○ **Good practice:** Practise safe online surfing, such as never divulging too much personal data, never opening attachments from people you do not know, as well as ensuring you have strong passwords on your accounts.

Did You Know?

Some Wi-Fi systems include an encryption system, such as WEP or WPA, to provide added security. Contact your Internet provider to make sure you are taking advantage of these.

MALWARE

By far the most common online threat comes from malware. In this section, we will examine the different types of malware more closely and explore how they work and the threats they pose.

MALICIOUS SOFTWARE

Malicious software has been around almost as long as computers. The first computer viruses were not deliberately made but came about from errors in software programs. These errors caused system crashes and became known as 'bugs'. However, people soon realized they could create their own bugs and even get them to self-replicate, and so the computer virus was born.

Who Creates them and Why?

You may wonder what sort of person would make malware and for what reason. The truth is, all sorts of people make malware and for all sorts of reasons.

- **Hackers**: People create malware to cause disruption and hack into high-profile computer systems, either just for fun of it or for some political agenda.

- **Criminals**: Malware Is used to steal data and money.

Right: Virus infections are an all-too-common threat.

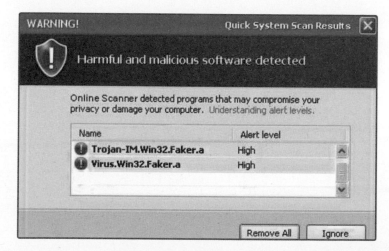

- **Businesses:** Some disreputable companies use malware to market products or get people to buy their software fixes.

- **Governments:** Even governments create malware to infiltrate the computers systems of another nation.

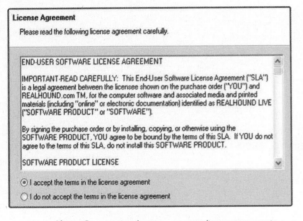

License Agreement

Please read the following license agreement carefully.

END-USER SOFTWARE LICENSE AGREEMENT

IMPORTANT-READ CAREFULLY: This End-User Software License Agreement ("SLA") is a legal agreement between the licensee shown on the purchase order ("YOU") and REALHOUND.com TM, for the computer software and associated media and printed materials (including "online" or electronic documentation) identified as REALHOUND LIVE ("SOFTWARE PRODUCT" or "SOFTWARE").

By signing the purchase order or by installing, copying, or otherwise using the SOFTWARE PRODUCT, YOU agree to be bound by the terms of this SLA. If YOU do not agree to the terms of this SLA, do not install this SOFTWARE PRODUCT.

SOFTWARE PRODUCT LICENSE

⦿ I accept the terms in the license agreement

○ I do not accept the terms in the license agreement

Above: By accepting the terms on some licence agreements, you are agreeing to have malware installed on your machine.

How They Get In

Malicious software can get into a computer in a number of ways: some are hidden in programs and are activated when you install the program; some software developers create free programs just in order to install malware on people's machines; while other malware is disguised as genuine files and is activated when you open the file. Additionally, some malware lingers on malicious websites, infecting your Internet browser when you visit the site.

Hot Tip

Whenever you install new software, especially free programs, always read the user agreement carefully and do a search on the Internet to see if other users have developed malware issues after installing.

WHAT IS OUT THERE?

Malware is a broad term and includes all sorts of malicious software that can range from being minor annoyances to programs that can erase all your data, steal your files or disable your computer. Sometimes infection by malware is obvious because you may lose data or suffer continuous computer crashes. However, with some malware, you may not even know you have been infected.

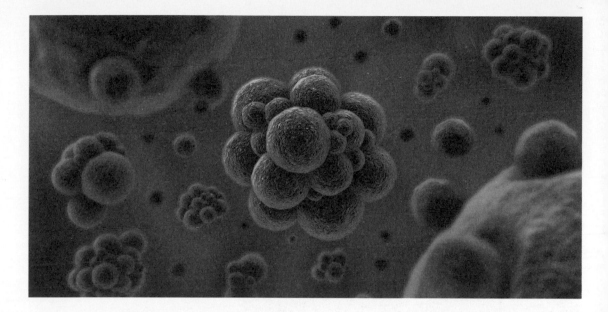

Computer Viruses

Most people have heard of computer viruses, but few people really understand how they work. Simply put, a computer virus is a piece of code that self-replicates and spreads to other computers. Viruses are normally written to have a specific purpose, such as deleting files or creating errors in software. A virus can enter a computer through various means, such as in email attachments or the programs you download, and they often infect other files on a computer, which allows the virus to spread when you pass these file on. Because of this, even the people who create viruses have no control over the number of machines a single virus can infect.

Right: Viruses can hide in programs or attachments.

Types of Computer Virus

Computer viruses come in various guises, and each one behaves differently.

○ **Program viruses:** These infect executable files (programs), and the virus is installed into the computer memory with the executable file, where it infects other files and acts out its programming.

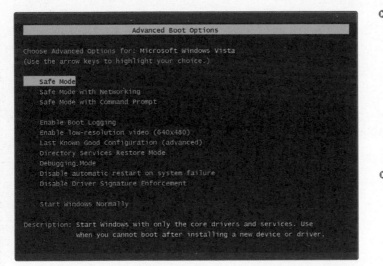

Above: Some viruses will prevent your PC from booting up normally.

○ **Boot viruses:** Rather than infecting computer memory, boot viruses infect the record used by operating systems when they start up, so the virus is reinstalled every time you turn on.

○ **Stealth viruses:** These viruses are designed to avoid detection. Commonly, this is done by preventing the section of hard disk they are on from being read.

○ **Polymorphic viruses:** Just as biological viruses mutate, so do polymorphic viruses, changing their source code with each infection to make detection and removal harder.

○ **Macro viruses:** These infect the macros (little pieces of code that do specific tasks) in program files, such as word-processing documents or spreadsheets.

○ **Active X viruses:** Active X is a framework used by software programs to share information, and by infecting this framework, Active X viruses can spread easily.

Worms

Similar to a computer virus, a worm can self-replicate and is designed to do harm. However, the big difference is in the way a worm spreads. Rather than infecting files that require human activity to pass them on, such as in email attachments, worms can spread over computer networks without assistance. When one computer on a network is infected, the worm will spread to all other machines on that network. Some worms have even been known to email themselves to everybody in a person's address book.

Above: The harm that worms can cause varies from simply consuming bandwidth, to deleting and encrypting files or worse.

Above: People use spyware and keyloggers to hack into online accounts.

Hot Tip

If you notice your computer is running unusually slowly, you may have inadvertently installed spyware, as it often runs in the background using system resources and slowing things down.

Spyware

Unlike a virus, spyware does not self-replicate. As its name suggests, the sole purpose of spyware is to spy on a person's computer activity. Spyware can collect all sorts of data about your computer use, such as the websites you visit, while some spyware, known as 'keyloggers', even records your keystrokes, which can be used to identify your passwords and usernames for online accounts.

Adware

While different to spyware, adware is often installed with it. Companies pay a lot of money to malware developers to have adware installed on people's machines. It works by sending specific advertisements to you depending on your web-browsing history. This may be in the form of pop-ups or it may replace your browser homepage and bookmarks. Other adware can even replace your search-engine results with websites from the people who have paid the adware developers.

Ransomware

Ransomware is designed solely to make money. It works by holding your computer or files hostage until you pay a ransom. Some ransomware will flash up warning messages telling you to pay money to get rid of the messages, hoping that the annoyance will be enough for you to cough up, while other ransomware, such as CryptoLocker, encrypts all your files so you cannot access them until you have paid to have them decrypted.

Scareware

Scareware is a less blunt method of obtaining money, where the malware creates a fake warning message suggesting your computer has been infected with a virus or spyware while suggesting you buy a particular malware removal product to solve the problem.

Trojan Horse

A Trojan horse does not describe a particular type of malware, such as spyware or virus, but describes a method of delivery. A Trojan horse is a piece of malware that is disguised as a legitimate file. Trojan horses can be spyware, or contain pieces of code that will join your

Above: Some ransomware not only locks your files, but also threatens to destroy them at a certain time.

computer to a botnet (we will discuss these in a minute). Trojan malware rarely replicates or spreads from machine to machine, as the purpose of a Trojan is to run in the background so a user does not know he or she has been infected.

Rootkit

Another type of malware that tries to remain hidden to avoid detection is the rootkit. A rootkit buries itself deep in the operating system much like a boot virus does, but they do not replicate or try to spread to other machines. Their purpose is to remain hidden so antivirus software and other security measures cannot detect them as they carry out the tasks they were programmed for. They are also notoriously difficult to remove.

Above: The best way to protect yourself from malware is to use antivirus programs.

Bots

As mentioned in the previous chapter, bots are computer codes designed to do a specific task. Bots are not necessarily malevolent; search engines, for instance, use bots to identify what is on a web page, but bots can be used maliciously, especially when they are working together (see below).

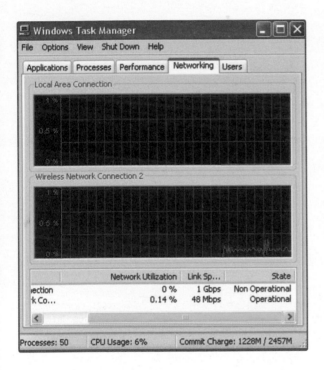

Botnets

Botnets are when large number of bots work together for a common goal. When a computer becomes part of a botnet, the bots function on people's computers in the background with the user often unaware. Botnets work together and can send out spam and other malware, or target specific networks or website servers, either to take them down or to bombard them with so many requests that the server becomes clogged, known as a distributed denial of service attack (DDoS).

Left: Unexplained network activity could mean you have become part of a botnet.

Hot Tip

If your Internet connection is running slowly, or you notice network activity even when you are not on the Internet, it could be because your machine may have become part of a botnet.

PROTECTING YOURSELF

As computers and the Internet get ever more sophisticated, so do viruses and malware. Antivirus developers are in a constant battle to identity and eliminate new threats. However, they are always one step behind the malicious coders. Antivirus software is crucial, but even with it installed, malware can still be a problem. Because of this, it is worth being prepared for the worst.

Backing Up

Data loss can be one of the worst outcomes from an attack by malware, so ensure you back up all your important files regularly. However, it is worth remembering that if a virus has been on your machine for a while, your backup files may also be infected. Do not just have one system for backing up either; think about using a cloud solution (online file storage) as well as a hardware system, such as a flash drive.

Above: Cloud storage solutions such as Dropbox can be used to store back-ups of your important files.

PC Health Checks

Regular use of diagnostic software (*see* pages 174–77) can help spot and eliminate threats before they cause harm. You can also take your computer to a trained professional for regular health checks.

Warning Others

If your system does become infected with malware, think about warning other people, such as those in your email address book, as you may have Inadvertently already spread the malware.

THE WORST OFFENDERS

Malware can often make the headlines, especially when it attacks high-profile organizations, or if it has become particularly widespread. Here are some famous examples of malware.

- **The Love Bug virus**: Perhaps the most successful computer virus attack in history, infecting an estimated 50 million computers. The virus was hidden in an email attachment purporting to be a love letter, triggering people to open it.

- **The Anna Kournikova worm**: The Kournikova worm was attached to an email claiming to have naked pictures of the tennis star. Once opened, the worm sent itself to everybody in a user's address book and infected tens of millions of machines.

- **Conficker Botnet**: In 2009 Conficker became the largest botnet ever and took control of millions of PCs around the world, yet to this day nobody knows for what purpose or by whom.

Left: Promises of naked pictures of Anna Kournikova were enough to convince millions of people to open an attachment containing a virus.

IDENTITY THEFT

Identity fraud is one of the fastest-growing crimes and it can cause chaos for its victims. Identity theft can result in somebody stealing from you, taking out loans in your name or even committing crimes while pretending to be you.

A CASE OF STOLEN IDENTITY

In 2006, when 24-year-old university graduate Victoria Sennitt opened her post, she was surprised to see a letter from a mobile phone company welcoming her to her new contract. Because Victoria had not signed up for a new mobile phone, she made some enquiries and was shocked to discover her identity had been stolen by fraudsters, who had used information she had left on social media websites to apply for a mobile phone.

'I know it sounds stupid,' Victoria told UK Newspaper The *Daily Mail*, 'but I feel very violated to know that a criminal was able to log on to my page and steal my personal details.'

Victoria was lucky; she managed to convince the phone company that it was a fraudster who had taken out the contract, but not everybody is so fortunate.

Above: Fraudsters may assume your identity in order to make purchases – for which you then receive the bill.

A Growing Problem

Identity theft is a huge problem. In the United States, it is estimated that identity theft costs Americans over $20 billion each year, and in the UK, identity fraudsters are stealing nearly £2 billion of other people's money. And the problem is getting worse.

Online Activity

Identity theft is not just an online problem; fraudsters can get hold of our personal information in other ways, such as going through our rubbish bins. However, the reason identity fraud is rising so quickly is because there is an increasing amount of information about us online, which has made it so much easier to get hold of our personal details. Using social media, email and other online platforms, fraudsters have ready access to all sorts of personal information about us, which they can use to commit fraud in our name.

CONSEQUENCES OF IDENTITY THEFT

Before we look at how identity fraudsters get hold of our personal information and what we can do about it, it is worth reiterating the consequences of having your identity stolen.

- **Financial:** Somebody assuming your identity can take out loans and other financial commitments under your name, for which you may be deemed liable.

- **Driving licence:** Your name could be used to obtain a driving licence, which could result in you being penalized for somebody else's driving infringements.

- **Benefits and tax:** An identity fraudster may use your name to claim State benefits or file fraudulent tax returns.

- **Passport:** Your identity may be used to obtain a passport, preventing you from getting one.

Above: With enough information, fraudsters can apply for credit cards in your name.

- **Crime:** Frauds or other crimes may be committed under your name, for which you could be held responsible if you cannot prove it was not you.

- **Credit score:** Your credit rating could be damaged, making it harder for you to get a loan, mortgage or credit card.

- **Reputation:** Somebody pretending to be you could say and do things on social media that may cause you embarrassment.

> ## Hot Tip
> Never divulge information over the Internet that could be used to steal your identity, especially your address, phone number, and bank and credit card details.

ASSUMING YOUR IDENTITY

Fraudsters employ a number of different tactics to get hold of your personal data online. These range from the very simple to some ingenious methods of fooling you to hand over information.

Social Media

Perhaps the places with the greatest wealth of personal information available for fraudsters to take advantage of are social media websites. People include all sorts of details on their Facebook, Twitter and LinkedIn profiles, feeds and pages, such as where they live, phone

Above: If you do not take precautions, fraudsters may use your personal information to obtain identity documents in your name or apply for credit cards.

numbers, email addresses, where they went to school, the name of their partners and where they work. On its own, this sort of information may not be enough to assume your identity. However, identity fraudsters piece together information from different social media sites and use other resources, such as electoral roles and telephone directories, to fill in the blanks.

Above: People include all sorts of personal information in their Facebook profiles, from addresses and phone numbers to their date of birth.

Phishing

Email can be another resource used by identity fraudsters to extract information about you. As we have already seen, phishing techniques are designed to fool you into sending information. Phishing can be a simple message, suggesting a company is updating its records and needs your address and phone number, to sophisticated scams where spoof websites are set up and you are sent a link to log on. Often, these websites look indistinguishable from the real thing. Phishing is not just a problem on email either. Twitter, Facebook and SMS text messages can all be used for phishing.

Did You Know?

Even innocent information posted on social media, such as the name of your children's school or the bus number you take to get to work, can be used by fraudsters to figure out your rough location and eventually your address.

Online Privacy

Even if you have your social media settings on the strictest privacy levels possible, or are only sending emails or direct messages to people you know and trust, you can never be sure that

Gmail
by Google

Dear Gmail User,

As part of our security measures, we regularly update all accounts on our database system. We are unable to update your email account and therefore we will be closing your email accounts to enable the web upgrade.

You have been sent this invitation because our records indicate you are currently a user whose account has not been activated. We are therefore you sending this email so you can inform us whether you still want to use this account. If you are still interested please confirm your account by updating your details immediately because out system requires an account verification for the update.

To prevent an interruption with your Gmail services, please take a few moments to update your account by filling out the verification and update form immediately.

Click here to verify your account

Above: Be wary of emails apparently from well-known companies asking you to verify your account; they are often phishing.

Hot Tip

If you are sent a link by email, one way to check that the link address is authentic is to hover your mouse over it and look on the bottom left-hand side of your Internet browser where the actual address is displayed.

shortener wherever you

compose a Tweet; some

3. Post the Tweet.

https://twitter.com

Above: When you hover over a link, you can see its actual address on the bottom left of your browser.

other people will not see what you have written. These days, people check their email and social media in all sorts of places, so you never know who could be looking over the shoulder of the person you are chatting to.

Hacking

Another method employed by fraudsters to gather information about you is to hack into your online accounts. We will discuss hacking in more detail and what you can do about it a little later.

Malware

Malware is another method employed by people to gather information about you in order to assume your identity. Keyloggers, spyware and viruses can be used to monitor what you are doing on the Internet or to steal files containing personal information from your computer.

IDENTIFYING IDENTITY FRAUD

The problem with identity fraud is the longer somebody gets away with it, the worse the consequences can be. For this reason, it is important to spot the signs early, so if there are any financial ramifications, they are kept to a minimum.

Monitoring Your Finances

Because of the prevalence and growing threat of identity fraud, it is important to check your personal finances regularly and be on the alert for unusual activity.

- **Not receiving bills**: If your usual bills or statements stop arriving, it could be a sign that someone has changed the account address.

- **Credit cards**: If you are sent credit cards that you did not apply for, somebody else may have ordered them in your name.

- **Statements**: Receiving financial statements from organizations you do not remember signing up to is a common sign of identity fraud.

- **Refusal of credit**: If you have been denied credit, it may be because somebody else has obtained credit in your name and damaged your credit history.

- **Statement items**: Anything on your bank or credit card statement that you do not remember purchasing needs investigating.

- **Phone calls**: Unexpected calls from debt collectors, financial organizations and banks can often be a sign that your identity has been stolen.

Hot Tip

Companies such as www.equifax.co.uk, www.experian.co.uk and www.checkmyfile.com can provide you with access to your credit history, which can help you spot if anybody is attempting to get credit in your name.

HSBC

Account Type :		BANK A/C
Account Name :		
Account Number :		
International bank account number :		
Branch identifier code :		

20 Jun		Balance brought forward			6450.06
22 Jun	VIS		11.46		6438.60
23 Jun	VIS		2000.00		4438.60
01 Jul	DD		10.00		
01 Jul	SO		5.00		4423.60
03 Jul	CR			39.00	
03 Jul	ATM		100.00		4362.60

Above: Make sure you check your bank and credit card statements for signs of identity theft.

PREVENTION IS BETTER THAN CURE

Before we look at what you can do if you think your identity has been stolen, it is worth looking at measures you can take to prevent identity fraud in the first place.

- **Never**: Reveal personal information over the Internet or email, such as your address, account numbers, phone numbers or passwords, even if you are sure of the person you are communicating with.

- **Always**: Keep your online passwords private. Remember to change them regularly and ensure they are as strong as possible.

- **Statements**: Make sure you shred any paper bills and statements. Do not simply throw them in the rubbish bin.

- **Emails**: If companies email you requesting personal information, insist they send the request by post (if they do not have your address, it is a sign they may not be who they say they are).

Above: Credit reference agencies can help you spot attempts at identity fraud.

HELP, MY IDENTITY HAS BEEN STOLEN!

If you suspect your identity has been stolen, it is important to act promptly in order to minimize the impact of the theft. If you spot any of the symptoms of identity fraud, follow these steps.

1. Contact your bank, building society or credit card company and explain your fears immediately. Ask for advice on freezing your account, getting replacement cards and changing passwords and PINs.

2. Contact the police. Identity theft is a crime and you may be able to recoup some or all of your losses if you report it and get a crime reference number.

3. Contact credit reference agencies, such as Experian and Equifax, and ask for advice on getting your credit rating repaired, as it may have been damaged by the identity fraudsters.

4. If you suspect your online accounts have been compromised, contact the companies concerned. Change passwords and other information that you use to log on.

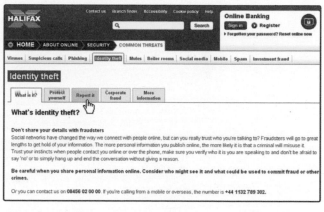

Above: Report identity theft as soon as you suspect it.

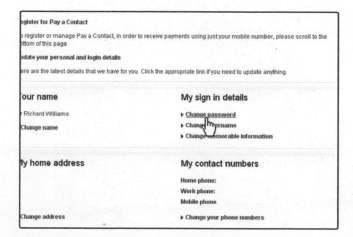

Above: Change your password.

HACKING

Hacking can affect people in different ways. Websites, personal computers and online accounts can all be hacked. Even some of the largest companies in the world fall foul of hackers, so what exactly can you do about it?

UNDERSTANDING HACKING

We discussed earlier the reasons people hack into computers, but it is worth looking at who is at risk, how to avoid being hacked in the first place and what you can do if you have been hacked.

What Can Be Hacked

When people think of computer hacking, they normally think of illicit computer experts breaking into government networks. However, hacking is quite a broad term and can describe a number of different methods of unauthorized computer use.

Above: Hackers can take over your online accounts and computers.

- **Network hacks:** Attacking entire computer networks is normally done by protestors, organized hacking groups and criminal gangs.

- **Personal computer hacking:** People gain access to personal computers to steal data or use them as part of a botnet.

- **Account hacking:** Perhaps the most common and simplest form of hacking is gaining access to somebody else's online account.

NETWORK HACKING

The most sophisticated form of hacking is when people break into high-profile computer networks, such as governmental organizations or big companies. The way hackers do this varies, from using highly sophisticated programming, software and equipment, to far simpler methods.

- **Vulnerabilities**: Exploiting holes in system security systems, such as outdated network log-in protocols.

- **Human weakness**: Taking advantage of bad security practices, such as users who have weak passwords.

- **Botnet attacks**: Using thousands of machines to bombard a network with attempts at access.

Did You Know?

In 2008, a USB flash drive was found in a car park outside a Department of Defense building. When a curious employee found it and plugged into a computer, it granted hackers access to the entire network.

GETTING YOU TO DO THE DIRTY WORK

One of the most common reasons people hack into personal computers is to take it over or make it part of a botnet so it can be used to do further hacking activities or distribute spam or malware.

Right: Be wary of using other people's flash drives or removable media.

DDoS Attacks

The simplest way hackers can attack a network server is by employing a Distributed Denial of Service attack (DDoS). This involves getting thousands or even millions of machines to access a server or website simultaneously, which causes an overload and prevents regular access. Because the requests are made from thousands of different machines, all from different locations with individual IP addresses, DDoS attacks are difficult to fix because system administrators cannot tell which computers are legitimate and which form part of the DDoS attack.

Zombie Computer

When a hacker or piece of malware has compromised a computer, it is referred to as a 'zombie computer'. This is because users are normally unaware their computer is being used for nefarious purposes.

This webpage is not available   chrome

Google Chrome could not load the webpage because **www.cia.gov** took too long to respond. The website may be down, or you may be experiencing issues with your Internet connection.

Here are some suggestions:

- Reload this webpage later.
- Check your Internet connection. Restart any router, modem, or other network devices you may be using.
- Add Google Chrome as a permitted program in your firewall's or antivirus software's settings. If it is already a permitted program, try deleting it from the list of permitted programs and adding it again.
- If you use a proxy server, check your proxy settings or contact your network administrator to make sure the proxy server is working. If you don't believe you should be using a proxy server, adjust your proxy settings: Go to **Applications > System Preferences > Network > Advanced > Proxies** and deselect any proxies that have been selected.

Error 7 (net::ERR_TIMED_OUT): The operation timed out.

Above: DDoS attacks cause websites to become unavailable.

Symptoms of a Zombie Computer

While hard to detect, having a PC turned into zombie computer does have some tell-tale signs. Trojans and bots will use your system resources, such as processor and Internet connection, slowing things down.

Common Symptoms of a Hacked Computer

◌ **Computer fan:** If your computer fan runs excessively when your computer is idle, it could be a sign that a malicious program is running (or a sign that your computer needs cleaning!).

◌ **Shut down:** If your computer takes longer than normal to shut down or will not shut down properly, it could be because of malicious programs.

- **Programs:** Slow programs and regular screen freezes can be caused by bots and Trojans running in the background.

- **Updates:** Some programs installed by hackers prevent you from updating operating systems and antivirus, as these can spot and remove the malicious code.

- **Internet connection:** If your computer is part of a botnet, it may be using your Internet connection, slowing other Internet use down.

System Resources

One of the best ways to identify that you have been hacked is to keep an eye on your system resources and see what processes are running or how much network access is being used.

Using Windows Task Manager

In Windows systems, you can access information about your system resources by using the Task Manager.

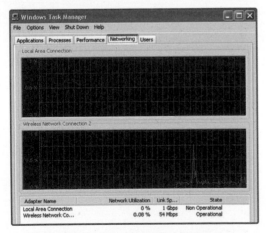

Above: Windows Task Manager processes.

Above: Look for spikes in network usage.

1. Close all programs and press **Ctrl**, **Alt**, **Delete** together.

2. In early Windows systems, such as XP, the Task Manager will pop straight up. In later versions of Windows (Windows 7 and Windows 8), you have to select it from a menu.

3. Click on the Processes tab to see what is running in the background. Look for cryptic names that could be malicious programs, and click on **Mem Usage** to see what is using the most resources.

4. Use the **Networking** tab to see if anything is accessing the Internet (if you are not using your connection, **Network Utilization** should be 0%).

> **Hot Tip**
> If you don't recognize the description of a process in the Task Manager, use Google or another search engine to find out what it does.

Hot Tip

Don't turn off or force quit processes you don't recognize, as it can make your computer unstable and could lead to data loss and system crashes.

Above: Use a search engine to help you identify the different processes in your Task Manager.

Using Activity Monitor

To check system resources on an OS X machine you use Apple's Activity Monitor.

1. Open your **Applications** folder and look for **Activity Monitor** in **Utilities**.

2. Use the **System Memory** tab to look at running processes and the **Network** tab to see what is accessing your Internet connection.

Removing Malicious Programs

We will discuss removing malicious programs used for hacking on pages 157–64 and 235–41, but it is worth noting that most OS providers include special automated tools for removing botnets and other malicious programs in their regular updates, which emphasizes the importance of ensuring your machine is kept up to date.

Above: Apple's Activity Monitor.

PREVENTING HACKERS

Prevention is better than cure, so ensure you are doing the following to minimize the risk of your machine being hacked:

- **Firewall**: Make sure you have a firewall installed and never turn it off; it is your first line of defence against hackers.

- **Antivirus**: Make sure your antivirus is always running and kept up to date.

- **Updating**: Keep your programs, especially your operating system, regularly updated.

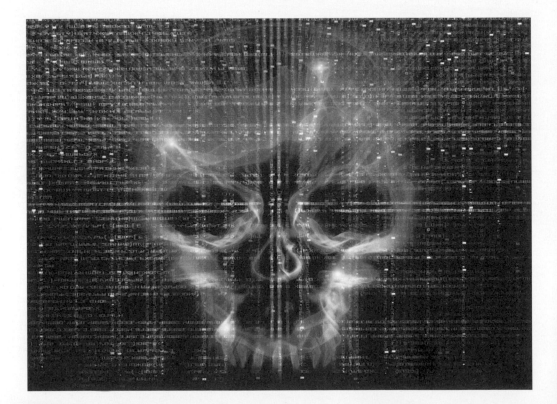

HACKED ONLINE ACCOUNTS

Your computer is not the only thing that is at risk from hackers. Online accounts can be hacked too. This is done for a number of reasons.

- **Identity theft**: Gaining access to your online accounts is a way for identity fraudsters to obtain personal information about you.

- **Crime:** Criminals can steal your money if they hack into your bank or credit card account.

- **Spam, malware and phishing**: Taking over a social media account is a good way to spread spam and malware, or to fool people into handing over information because they think the message comes from a trusted source.

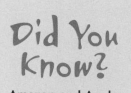

Did You Know?

Amazon and Apple have now addressed the security flaws that enabled hackers to take over Mat Honan's online accounts.

An Extreme Example

In 2012, technology writer Mat Honan became the victim of online hackers who took over nearly all his online accounts. After taking advantage of a security flaw on an online retail site, Amazon, hackers were able to use the information they found to delete Mat's emails, take over his Google and Twitter accounts, as well as erase all data from his Apple devices.

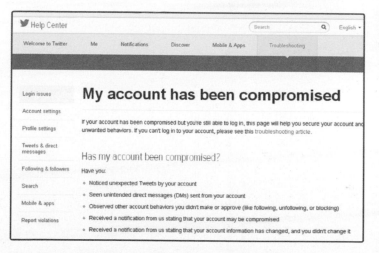

Above: Social media platforms such as Twitter are common targets for hackers.

HOW HACKERS GAIN ACCESS

Hackers can use all sorts of information about you to gain access to your online account. These are the most common means.

- **Passwords:** Weak passwords that are easy to guess are one of the easiest ways hackers gain access to your online accounts.

- **Personal information:** Hackers sometimes use personal information they find online about you, such as your address or phone number, to convince an online account that they are you and have lost their password.

- **Spyware:** Keyloggers and other spyware can give hackers access to your usernames and passwords.

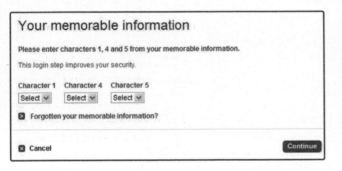

Above: Banks often have extra layers of security, such as asking you for memorable information before you can log in.

Account Security

Some online accounts are far more secure than others. Banks, for instance, have several layers of identity authentication, including passwords, PINs and memorable questions. However, social media, email and online retail sites have fewer layers, making them easier targets for online hackers.

EMAIL ACCOUNTS

Taking over your email account is not only a severe invasion of privacy, but it also allows hackers to send spam, malware or phishing emails to everybody in your address book, who may think the message is from you. In addition, having access to your email account can let a hacker reset your passwords on online accounts, granting them access.

Securing Your Email Account

Protecting your email account from hackers is crucial, so make sure your account is secure.

- **Security measures:** Choose a secure email provider, preferably one that has several layers of verification, such as SMS or phone verification. If these are optional, take advantage of them.

- **Password:** Choose a strong password and change it regularly, and never tell anybody your email password.

- **Security measures:** React quickly to messages about possible attempts to hack your email account. However, be wary of phishing messages claiming to be from your email provider.

Above: Take advantage of the extra security features offered by your email account provider.

- **Multiple accounts:** Think about using more than one email address.

Symptoms of an Email Hack

Determining if your email account has been hacked is not easy; often hackers want to remain undetected, so they go to extreme lengths to hide their presence. However, there can be some tell-tale signs.

Hot Tip

Be careful when accessing email in a public place. Make sure nobody is looking over your shoulder and never tick the 'Remember my password' box on a computer that is not yours.

○ **Sent messages:** Hackers often delete the messages they send to avoid detection, so if your sent messages folder is empty or you spot messages that you did not send, you may have been hacked.

Above: Delivery-failure notifications for emails you do not remember sending are a sign that you have been hacked.

○ **Non-delivery reports:** If your account has been used to send random emails and spam, you may get non-delivery reports that have been sent to accounts no longer in existence.

○ **Friends/colleagues:** People in your address book may ask if you sent them a recent message, as they may be suspicious about its content.

SOCIAL MEDIA

Social media platforms are perhaps the most easily and often hacked accounts. Quite often, people use social media accounts to send spam or direct a user's friends and followers to a website, but a hacked social media account can bring with it other problems, such as somebody getting hold of personal information, which can be used to hack into other accounts or as part of an identity fraud.

Above: Take advantage of the security and privacy settings on your social media accounts.

Securing Your Social Media Accounts

As with your email account, it is important to use a strong password to access your social media platforms, such as Twitter, Facebook or LinkedIn, but there are a couple of things you can do to secure your account.

- **Privacy and security settings**: Take advantage of the platform's privacy and security measures. (*See* pages 108–12 for more information.)

- **Avoid**: Revealing personal information on social media. Even if you think you are only talking to friends, you never know if their accounts have been compromised.

> **Hot Tip**
> Beware of messages on Twitter alerting you to a link of a picture, video or something that somebody has written about you on the Internet. This is a common sign an account has been hacked and the link might take you to a malicious website.

Symptoms Your Social Media Has Been Hacked

The most common sign your social media account has been hacked is when your friends and followers start receiving messages from you that you did not send. You may also have started following or befriending a lot of new people. Make sure you regularly check your activity so you can spot a hack as soon as possible.

FINANCIAL ACCOUNTS

Arguably the most damaging type of online account to have hacked is one that deals with financial transactions. Not only can somebody access your money if they hack into your online bank or credit card accounts, but some retail accounts hold other personal information, such your credit card details, address, email and phone number, which a hacker may gain access to.

Above: Some online retailers, such as Amazon, hide your credit card details in case your account is hacked.

Tell-tale Signs of a Hacked Financial Account

The last thing you want a hacker to have access to is your money, be it via an online retailer, bank or other financial institution. Fortunately, most financial organizations and ecommerce websites take security seriously, but it is important to look out for tell-tale signs of a breach.

- **Log in**: If you cannot log in, it could be because the account has been hacked. Contact the online account provider immediately.

- **Warnings**: Most financial organizations will send you a warning if they suspect unusual behaviour on your account.

- **Statements**: Check your bank and credit card statements carefully. If you spot a transaction you do not remember, investigate it.

- **Orders**: Regularly check your order history on retail and ecommerce websites for any new items.

CALENDAR	SEARCH: order	

Delete   ← ⟨⟨ →   Move ▾   Spam ▾   Actions ▾

Thank you for your order, richard

Order Ref No.: 1086240
Ordering Information:
E-mail Address:

Invoice Address:
R N Williams

GB Mainland

Delivery details:
richard williams

Above: Order confirmations can be a sign somebody has hacked one of your accounts.

- **Emails**: Websites may send you an email alerting you to a product that has been dispatched, or to confirm that you have changed some personal details.

- **Balance**: Make sure you know your account balance. If it is not what it should be, investigate it.

HELP, MY ACCOUNT HAS BEEN HACKED!

If any of your online accounts have been hacked, whether social media, email or a bank or ecommerce site, it is crucial to act as quickly as possible to minimize the damage. If you think your account has been hacked, take the following steps.

1. Inform the website or account provider immediately. If you cannot log in, contact them by telephone for help, not by email.

2. Change your password and other log-in information, such as your email address,

3. Check your personal information has not been changed.

4. Change your password on other websites in case they have also been compromised. Check these for signs of hacking.

5. If your online account contains credit card or bank account numbers, tell your financial institutions immediately.

Above: If you think an account has been hacked, check your personal information has not been changed.

Above: Change your password on other accounts.

Hot Tip

If somebody has committed fraud by hacking into one of your online accounts, contact the police and report it. You may need a crime reference number to get the money back.

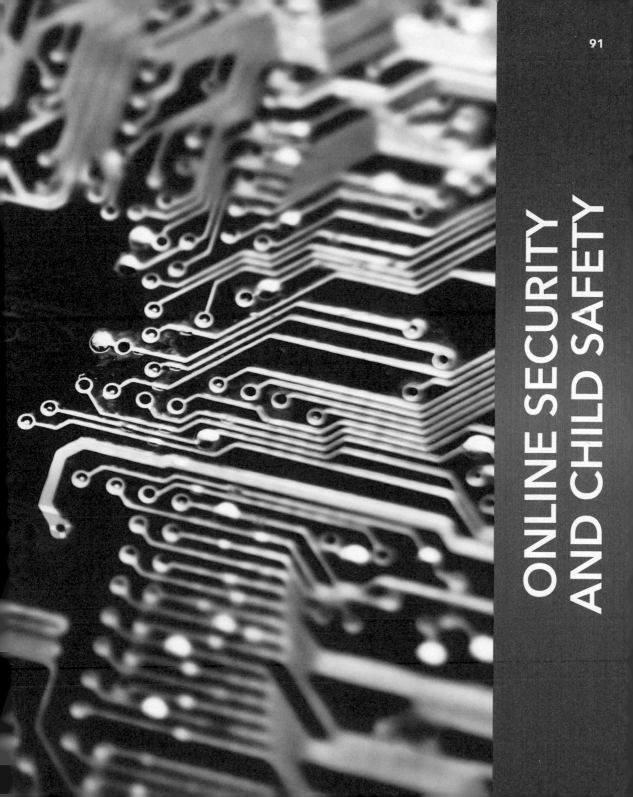

ONLINE SECURITY AND CHILD SAFETY

WEB BROWSING SECURITY

Web browsers provide us access to the World Wide Web, but you can also use them to keep you safe online. In this section, we will explore how web browsers interact with websites and how the various features and functions can protect us online.

WEB NAVIGATION

When we think of websites, we often think in terms of 'visiting' a web page. However, this is not strictly accurate. When we enter a website address into our browser or click on a link, our web browser connects with the server hosting the website and downloads all the information to our computers. In other words, we are not visiting a website, but the website is visiting us. This is why it is important to have Internet security systems such as antivirus software and firewalls, because we are allowing all this data onto our machines.

HTML

Web pages function using HTML (HyperText Markup Language), which provides the content of a web page and defines how the web browser should display it.

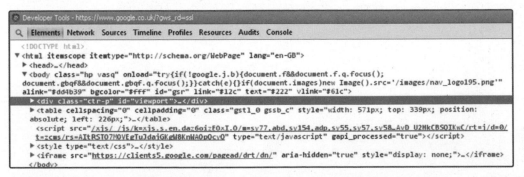

Above: A web page is made up of HTML code.

Browser Interaction

Not only do web browsers download information from a web server to our computers, but they also provide information the other way. To understand the sorts of security issues that can arise from web browsing, it is important to understand the sorts of information we are inadvertently handing over each time we visit a web page.

- **IP address:** When we visit a website, our browser tells the web server the IP address of our computer, which allows the website to know where to send the page.

- **System information:** In order to ensure the web page is presented correctly, web browsers provide information relating to the computer environment we are using, such as the operating system and browser type.

- **Linked page:** If you have visited a page from a search engine or link, the web browser will also provide this information to a web server.

Right: Services such as Google maps use our IP address to identify our location.

Did You Know?

Websites can use your IP address to discern your approximate location. This helps some services, such as search engines, to offer you results based on where you live.

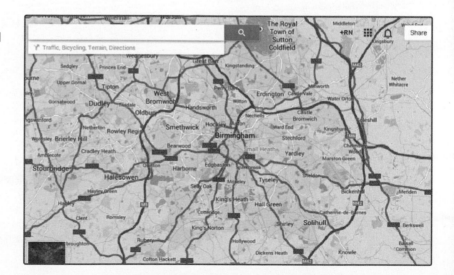

STORING INFORMATION

When we visit a website, our Internet browsers also store information on our computers about our interaction.

○ **History:** Your browser stores a history of every page that you visit, including the date and time of your visit.

○ **Cache:** Your browser temporarily stores certain aspects of web pages on your computer, such as images and HTML. This helps speed up the loading of the web pages you visit more frequently.

○ **Forms, searches and passwords:** Your browser may also retain passwords and usernames for different sites, as well as information you include in forms.

Clearing Browser Data In Internet Explorer 9

To clear your web-browsing history in Internet Explorer:

1. In the **Tools** menu choose **Safety**.

2. Click **Delete browsing history**.

Delete Browsing History

☑ **Temporary Internet files**
Copies of webpages, images, and media that are saved for faster viewing.

☑ **Cookies**
Files stored on your computer by websites to save preferences such as login information.

☑ **History**
List of websites you have visited.

☐ **Form data**
Saved information that you have typed into forms.

☐ **Passwords**
Saved passwords that are automatically filled in when you sign in to a website you've previously visited.

☐ **InPrivate Blocking data**
Saved data used by InPrivate Blocking to detect where websites may be automatically sharing details about your visit.

☑ **Preserve favorite website data**
Keep cookies and temporary Internet files that enable your favorite websites to retain preferences and display faster.

About deleting browsing history   Delete   Cancel

Left: Deleting browser history.

3. Select the types of history you want to delete, such as browsing history and/or temporary Internet files (cache).

4. You can retain the cache just for your most-visited websites, by checking the **Preserve Favorites website data** box.

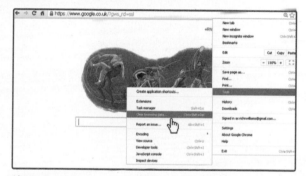

Above: When using Chrome, pressing Ctrl, Shift and N brings up the incognito window.

Hot Tip

If you do not want your web browser to record your page history, some browsers offer 'private', 'incognito' or 'anonymous' browsing options.

Above: Clearing browser data in Chrome.

Clearing Browser Data in Chrome

To clear your web history in Chrome:

1. Click the Chrome menu on the browser toolbar (the three horizontal stripes).

2. Select **Tools**, and then **Clear browsing data**.

3. A window will appear, providing you with a list of checkboxes for the types of information you wish to remove.

Above: Choose what history to delete.

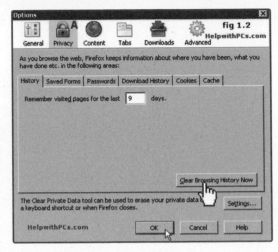

Above: Clearing history in Firefox.

Clearing Browser Data in Firefox

1. Click the menu button (three horizontal stripes).

2. Choose **History** and then **Clear browsing history**.

3. Select how far back you want to delete your history, or choose **everything**.

4. Select what information you want to erase, such as browsing history, cache or cookies.

COOKIES

Not only do our web browsers store information about our visit to a web page, but websites do so too. In order to improve our user experience, websites store information in cookies. Cookies are simply pieces of code stored on our computers. Generally, cookies do not pose too much of a security threat. However, if you would rather not have them on your system, you can also clear cookies in a similar way as clearing web-browsing history.

> ## Hot Tip
>
> We have included instructions for clearing web history in the most popular browsers. In other browsers or older versions of the ones listed, search for the right option by opening the settings panels.

Clearing and Blocking Cookies

You can clear, restrict and permit cookies in web browsers:

- **Internet Explorer:** Select the **Cookies** check box when deleting browser history.
- **Firefox:** Follow the instructions for clearing web history.

- **Chrome:** Go into the **Settings** menu (three horizontal stripes), click the **advanced settings** link and clicking **Content settings** under **Privacy**.

ANONYMOUS BROWSING

Even if you are blocking cookies or using a private browsing session, websites will still know your IP address because it is needed to deliver content to you. However, it is possible to visit websites anonymously by using an intermediary service, known as a proxy server.

Proxy Servers

A proxy server is a server located between you and the website you want to visit. When you connect using a proxy server, a website sees only the details of the proxy. However, using a proxy server is not without its risks. Some proxy servers are set up to entrap people, for example sending you to websites that look like your bank or email provider but which are, in fact, fake phishing web pages. Therefore, if you intend to use a proxy server, you need to ensure it is trusted. Websites such as www.publicproxyservers.com can help you find a proxy.

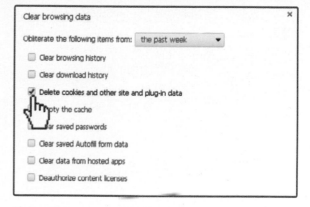

Above: Deleting cookies in Chrome.

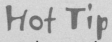

Hot Tip

Some websites such as www.kproxy.com and www.hidemyass.com offer anonymous browsing without the need of a proxy server. You can also download anonymous browser programs such as Tor (www.torproject.org).

Above: The Tor Project provides a completely anonymous browser.

Above: Connections in Internet properties.

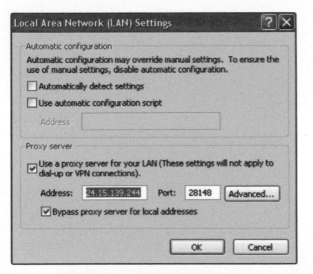

Above: Entering a proxy address and port number.

Using A Proxy Server On Windows

1. To use a proxy server, open **Internet Options** in your Control Panel.

2. Select **Network and Internet Connections**.

3. Click **Internet Options** and select **Connections**.

4. Choose **LAN Settings**.

5. Under **Proxy server**, select the **Use a proxy server for your LAN** check box.

6. Enter the IP address of the proxy server and port number, and click **OK**.

Hot Tip

For information on browsing more privately on mobile devices, such as smartphones or tablets, see the section on Wireless and Bluetooth Security on pages 193–200.

Using a Proxy Server on OS X

1. Choose **System Preferences** in the Apple menu.

2. Select **Network, Advanced,** and then click **Proxies**.

3. Choose the type of proxy, such as FTP (most common), and type its address and port number.

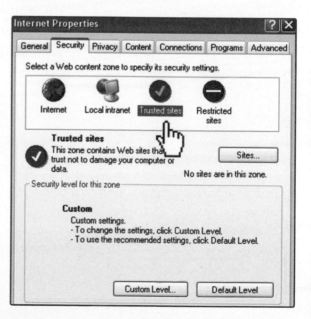

Above: Proxies menu.

BROWSER SECURITY SETTINGS

Web browsers include all sorts of other features that you can use to protect you from threats when you are surfing the Internet. However, adjusting these settings may reduce your user experience on certain websites.

○ **Cookies:** You can clear cookies from your system or prevent certain websites from installing them.

○ **Tracking:** You can prevent websites from tracking your activity.

○ **Private browsing:** You can stop the browser from storing your search history, page history and passwords.

Above: In Internet Explorer, you can assign security zones for trusted websites and those you would rather restrict.

○ **Location:** You can request that websites should not know your physical location, although some websites can ignore this request.

○ **Security zones:** Some browsers let you assign security zones to websites, where you can block certain content and restrict sites that are not trusted.

○ **Extensions and apps:** You can install and remove extensions and applications that extend the functionality of the web browser.

○ **Passwords and forms:** You can choose whether to allow the browser to remember passwords and information you use in online forms.

PHISHING AND MALWARE PROTECTION

Many Internet browsers now contain some form of malicious content protection. These normally warn you that a web page you are about to visit has been reported as containing malicious content, such as phishing or malware. This sort of protection is normally on when you install an Internet browser, and while you can usually turn it off in your browser settings, it is highly recommended that you leave it on.

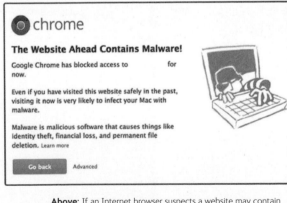

Above: If an Internet browser suspects a website may contain malicious software, it will flash up a warning message.

Antivirus Plug-ins

Some antivirus software can install a small program in your Internet browser called a plug-in. These can help you identify malicious websites when you are surfing the Internet or using search engines so they can warn you if you are about to download a file that has been reported as containing malware. For more information on this, see page 161.

WEBSITE SECURITY

Your browser is not the only form of security you can use when surfing the World Wide Web. Many websites implement security measures to keep you safe when you are online.

Secure Sockets Layer (SSL)

Websites that transmit sensitive information often employ a security mechanism called SSL (Secure Sockets Layer). This software secures an encrypted link between you and the web server, preventing anybody from intercepting any transmitted data.

SSL Certificates

Electronic certificates are used to verify the authenticity of secure SSL websites. These certificates tell browsers that the website can be trusted and are verified by third-party organizations. If you try to access a website that has a certificate that cannot be

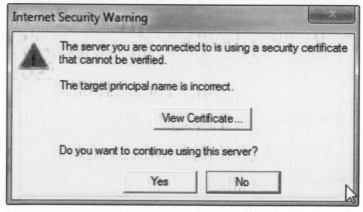

Above: SSL certificate warning.

verified, you will receive a message warning you not to proceed. Sometimes the problem is just a website error, perhaps caused by a certificate that has expired, but it is advisable not to proceed unless you are sure the website can be trusted.

HTTPS

You can tell if a website requires an SSL connection because it usually starts with HTTPS (HyperText Transfer Protocol Secure) rather than the standard HTTP. Some web browsers display a padlock icon in the address bar if a website is using HTTPS protocol.

Hot Tip

If you come across a security threat, you can report it to Google at www.google.co.uk/safebrowsing/report _badware/, helping to make searching on the Internet safer for everybody.

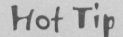

Web   Videos   News   Shopping   Images   More ▾   Search too

About 1,460,000,000 results (0.39 seconds)

Example Domain
www.example.com/ ▾
This site may harm your computer.
Example Domain. This domain is established to be used for illu
documents. You may use this domain in examples without prio
for permission. More information...

Where does email sent to *@example.com go? - Server Fa
serverfault.com/questions/.../where-does-email-sent-to-example-com-go ▾

Above: A warning on Google that a website may harm your computer.

SEARCH ENGINE SECURITY

Some search engines, such as Google and Bing, also have several useful security functions that can help keep you safe when looking for websites on the Internet.

- **Safe searching**: You can filter explicit content from all search results (to understand how to use this feature, see the section on parental controls on pages 129–33).

- **Signing in**: Requires you to sign in before you can access the search engine.

- **Malicious content warnings**: If a website is suspected of harbouring malicious content, there may be a warning next to it in the search engine results.

EMAIL SECURITY

Whether you use an online webmail service or download your emails to your computer using programs such as Outlook, you can use various security features to help keep you safe. You can often adjust these security features by logging on to your email provider and going into the settings menu.

- **Security information**: Add additional security information to your account, such as an alternative email address, mobile phone number or security question.

- **HTTPS**: Some webmail providers such as Gmail offer HTTPS for added security.

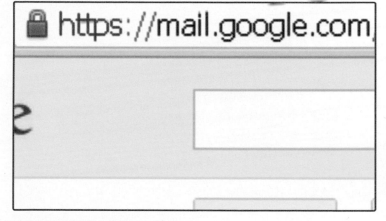

- **Blocked content**: Email providers may block images, attachments or other elements of an email if they appear to pose a threat.

Above: Google Mail uses HTTPS for added security.

- **Spam filters**: Most email providers have some form of spam filter that can recognize not only spam, but also phishing content.

- **Antivirus scanning**: Some email services have their own antivirus scanners that can be used when downloading attachments.

- **Reporting**: Most email providers let you report malicious content, phishing and spam emails; doing so helps improve their security for all their users.

SAFER SURFING TIPS

Now you know how websites operate and understand some of the features available to help you safely surf the Internet, it is worth looking at how you interact with the World Wide Web and what you can do to limit Internet security threats.

- **Personal information:** Never give out personal information unless you are sure you are on a verified, secure and safe website.

- **Security and privacy settings:** Take advantage of the security and privacy settings provided to you by web browsers, websites and email providers.

- **Password safety:** Never share passwords, ensure they are as strong as possible and change them regularly.

- **Unsecured or unknown websites:** Be wary of using websites that are not HTTPS for any financial transactions.

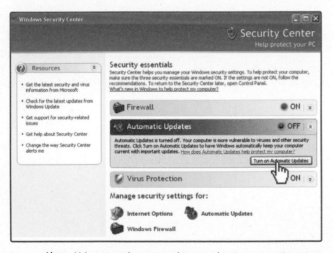

Above: Make sure you have your updates turned on in your operating system.

- **Links:** Avoid clicking links in emails, as they may not be genuine. Always type addresses in the URL bar or use search engines such as Google to find the websites you are looking for.

- **Keep up to date:** Keep your browsers and security software up to date, as well as your operating system and any programs that access the Internet.

SOCIAL MEDIA SECURITY

The way we communicate has changed for ever. Social media has made keeping in touch and meeting new people so much easier, but it has also opened us up to a range of new threats to our privacy and security.

THE SOCIAL MEDIA REVOLUTION

Facebook has over one billion users worldwide, Twitter over 250 million, and email is now far more popular than postal mail as a means of communication. This has meant a dramatic shift in the way we communicate. However, when it comes to what we say and to whom we speak, many of us are still stuck in the old ways, and forget that what we post on the Internet can often be seen by almost anybody.

Anybody and Everybody

One of the most common mistakes people make when using social media is assuming that they are only speaking to their friends and followers. However, this is rarely the case. While you can implement all sorts of privacy settings on social media websites, you can never be certain your content will stay private.

Right: There are countless social media platforms available.

SOCIAL MEDIA PLATFORMS

Social media has been around for some time, and while it is impossible to list all the available platforms, some social media sites are more popular than others.

Above: Facebook now has over a billion users.

Above: You can send up to 140 characters in a Tweet, but you can also attach images.

- **Facebook:** The world's most popular social networking site with over one billion members.

- **Twitter:** The platform that allows you to send 140-character messages, known as Tweets (a form of 'microblogging').

- **LinkedIn:** Used by professionals and those in the business world to network and connect with other professionals.

- **Pinterest:** Lets users collect and share photos of their favourite events, interests and hobbies.

- **Google Plus+:** Google's own social networking platform that interacts with many of Google's other services.

- **Tumblr:** Another microblogging platform, which allows users to share videos and other multimedia.

THE INFORMATION YOU PROVIDE

When we sign up to a social media account, we often provide all sorts of information. Social media providers keep some of this private, such as our email address and password, but other information ends up as part of our profile and may be visible to anyone.

Access to Information

Websites such as Twitter and Facebook now allow interaction from all sorts of apps and other websites. One of the consequences of this is that when are logged into a Twitter or Facebook account, all sorts of information about you can be accessed by third-party websites, such as your name, profile photo and even your interests.

Hot Tip

Never post anything on social media that you would find embarrassing if your parents, employers or some other such person were to see it, as you can never be sure they will not.

Ownership

Another aspect of social media that people often fail to understand is that we do not have ownership over the content we post. When we sign up to social media platforms, we often grant these websites the rights to do what they like with our content, which means we have no control over who has access to our images and videos.

SHARING INFORMATION

Whether you are sending Tweets, updating your Facebook wall or just creating a social media profile, it is important to understand what information should be shared and what could put you at risk from identify fraud or other security threats.

Sensitive Information

Sensitive information is anything that could be used by scammers, fraudsters and other types of people with dubious motives. Even information that may seem mundane can be used against us. Sensitive information falls into several categories.

○ **Identification:** Anything that can be used to identify who you are, such as your full name, names of children, spouses or other family members, and your date of birth.

○ **Location:** Anything that helps identify your address, such as the street in which you live or postcode.

○ **Security:** Passwords, account numbers and personal email addresses should never be divulged on social media.

○ **Schedules:** Details of when we are at home or at work, planned holidays and trips can all put us at risk.

Above: For security reasons passwords are normally obscured by asterisks when you log into social media.

PRIVACY SETTINGS

In order to control who sees what information, most social media websites have privacy settings, which you can adjust to allow certain information to be visible only to your friends and followers. While we cannot explain the settings of every social media platform in this book, we will look at how to increase security on the largest platforms – Facebook and Twitter.

FACEBOOK SECURITY AND PRIVACY

Facebook is the world's most popular social media platform, allowing over a billion people to share information with friends and family. However, you may not want everything about you to be known to just anybody, so it is important to try to control what you give out and who gets to see it.

Facebook Settings

In order to protect your personal information, Facebook provides all sorts of settings.

1. To access your security and privacy settings, click on the downward-pointing arrow in the top-right corner.

2. Click **Settings**.

3. Select **Security** in the menu on the left to adjust your security settings, and **Privacy** to adjust your privacy settings.

> ### Hot Tip
> When you sign up to Facebook, you are asked for a lot of information, but much of this is optional. Beyond your name, email address, birthday and gender you do not need to divulge anything else.

Facebook Security

In the security menu, you can adjust aspects of your account to make it more secure. Simply click **edit** next to each setting.

○ **Login notifications:** Receive email or text notifications if somebody tries to log into your account.

○ **Login approval:** Set a security code for logging in from a computer other than your own.

○ **Code generator:** Generate codes in your Facebook mobile app for logging in and resetting your password.

Right: Selecting Facebook settings.

○ **App passwords**: Create passwords for apps that cannot use security codes.

○ **Trusted contacts**: Allows you to choose trusted friends to help you get into a locked account.

○ **Trusted browser**: Select what browsers you can use to access your account.

○ **Where you're logged in**: Limit the locations where you can log in.

Facebook Privacy

In the privacy, timeline and blocking menus, you can control who sees what in your timeline, prevent people from tagging images of you, as well as block people with whom you would rather not engage.

○ **Who can see my stuff**: You can choose whether your posts are public or for friends only, and even restrict things you have already posted.

○ **Who can contact me**: Filter messages sent to you and who can send you a friend request.

○ **Who can look me up**: Edit who can search for your profile on both Facebook and in search engines.

○ **Timeline and tagging**: You can adjust who can post to your timeline, who can see things on it, as well as control who tags you in their posts and photos.

○ **Blocking**: Lets you block or restrict friends, apps and invitations.

> ## Hot Tip
> Never post a compromising picture on social media, even if it is meant for a select few to see, as you may find that you have no control over the number of times it is copied and reposted.

TWITTER SECURITY AND PRIVACY

While not as popular as Facebook, Twitter is still used by millions of people and has the potential to compromise your online security if you do not control the information you give out.

Twitter Profile

Twitter does not ask for as much personal information as Facebook, and it is entirely up to you how much information you want to make public on your Twitter profile. For most people, their profile contains their name and a short biography. However, some people have their location visible on their profile, as well as other sensitive information. Be careful when you compose your profile that you are not giving away too much personal detail.

Tweeting

The biggest threat to privacy and security on Twitter comes in what you talk about. Divulging too much information in a Tweet may mean the information gets into the wrong hands, and while Tweets drop down your timeline very quickly, they can remain accessible for months, even years.

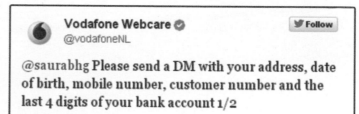

> **Vodafone Webcare** ✓ @vodafoneNL   🐦 Follow
>
> @saurabhg **Please send a DM with your address, date of birth, mobile number, customer number and the last 4 digits of your bank account 1/2**
>
> 2:08 PM - 17 Jan 2014

Above: Do not give out personal information in a Tweet, even if it appears to be a reputable company asking for it.

Twitter Settings

1. To access Twitter's security and privacy settings, click the gear icon in the top right-hand corner.

Above: Selecting settings in Twitter.

2. Click **Settings** in the drop-down menu.

3. Select **Security and Privacy** in the left-hand menu.

Twitter Security and Privacy

You can adjust several aspects of your account to protect your personal information.

- **Login verification:** Have Twitter send you an email or text whenever somebody attempts to log into your account.

- **Password reset:** Allows you to set Twitter to request additional information for resetting passwords.

- **Photo tagging:** As with Facebook, you can prevent people tagging you in photos.

- **Tweet privacy:** Choose to make your Tweets public, so anyone can see them, or private and visible only to your followers.

- **Tweet location:** Choose whether your location is included in your Tweets.

- **Discoverability:** Choose whether people can search for you on Twitter using your email address.

- **Promoted content:** Prevent Twitter from tailoring adverts specifically to you based on your Tweets and the people you follow.

> ### Hot Tip
> Avoid clicking on links from people you do not know on social media, as spammers often use these platforms to try to get you to visit websites with malicious content.

ONLINE HARASSMENT

As useful as social media is for helping us to socialize and connect with new people, it has given rise to a darker phenomenon – online harassment. Online bullying is not just something that children suffer from, as some people take great pleasure in abusing and making other people's lives a misery, no matter how old they are, and with social media, these people have an almost unlimited supply of victims.

Trolls

People who harass others online are known as trolls. Trolling can come in various forms.

- **Abuse:** Trolls often send people abusive messages.

- **Threats:** Some trolls threaten people with violence.

Above: Anyone can be subject to nasty comments or harassment online.

- **Cyberstalking**: Some trolls follow people around the Internet and harass them on different platforms.

- **Privacy**: People posting private information about you on social media is also a form of trolling.

Above: You can report somebody for abuse on Twitter using the settings menu in their profile.

Above: You can report somebody for abuse on Facebook via the '...' menu in their timeline.

Dealing with Trolls

The best way to deal with trolls is to block interactions with them and report their behaviour to the social media administrators. If trolls are making serious threats of violence towards you, you should consider contacting the police.

Reporting Abusive Behaviour

Most social media platforms have some facility for reporting abusive behaviour.

- **Facebook:** The best way to report abusive content or spam on Facebook is by using the Report link that appears near the content itself.

- **Twitter**: You can report abusive behaviour at the following address – https://support.twitter.com/forms/abusiveuser

- **LinkedIn:** Has a contact form for reporting abusive behaviour – https://help.linkedin.com/app/ask/path/rhsc

- **Pinterest**: You can report abuse and harassment using the contact form at http://help.pinterest.com/en/contact

- **Google Plus+**: Click on the arrow to the top and right of the post and select **Report abuse**.

- **Tumblr**: The only way to report abuse on Tumblr is to email the support desk – support@tumblr.com

> **Hot Tip**
> Never assume that private information and messages sent to friends and followers will remain private. You never know what other people will do with your information or how secure their web habits are.

SENSIBLE SOCIAL MEDIA USE

When using any social media website or app, it is a good idea to bear in mind some basic principles.

- **Sensitive information**: Avoid giving out any information that could be used by identity fraudsters, spammers or hackers.

- **Privacy**: No matter what security and privacy settings you have set, never say anything you would not want the whole world to hear.

- **Remember**: Something you say on social media could be accessible for weeks, months and even years into the future.

- **Passwords**: Guard your passwords, ensure they are strong and remember to change them regularly.

- **Connect**: Be careful whom you befriend or follow on social media. Not everyone will be who they say they are.

Above: Be careful about what pictures you post online.

- **Pictures:** Photos can be copied and forwarded easily, so never post any pictures that you would not feel comfortable letting the whole world see.

- **Links:** Do not click on links from people you do not know, as they may lead you to a malicious website.

- **Social media mobile apps:** See pages 203–05 about using apps and the risks they pose.

COMMON SOCIAL MEDIA SCAMS

Due to its popularity, social media has become a tempting target for scammers and fraudsters. Be on the lookout for some of these common scams.

- **Secret details about ...**: Often followed by the name of celebrity and including a link to tempt you to some salacious gossip, but which in fact leads you to a malicious site.

- **Help, need money**: Be wary of anybody asking for financial help. Often the fraudsters claim to be a victim of a terrible tragedy.

- **Did you see this picture of you?**: Watch out for any Tweets or Facebook messages containing a link to a picture of you. It normally directs you to a fake login screen designed to get your account details.

- **Ur cute. Message me**: Be wary of strangers claiming they find you attractive, as they are liable to be fraudsters.

Right: Beware of messages suggesting there is a compromising picture of you on the Internet somewhere.

> ## Hot Tip
>
> Government authorities, prospective employers and law-enforcement agencies commonly do searches on social media websites, so always think about what you are posting and who might see it in the future.

You have a new direct message.

Did you see this pic of you? lol bit.ly/UAzOu2 ...
07:13 AM - 30 Jan 13

Keep the conversation going.   Message

THE INTERNET AND CHILDREN

In many cases, teenagers and even young children know more than their parents when it comes to using the Web. However, they are vulnerable to some specific online risks, which will obviously vary depending on their age and Internet access. Let's first look at what these risks are.

THE TECH GENERATION

For many adults, the Internet and World Wide Web were not around when they grew up, which has meant the Internet is something we have had to learn as it developed. For youngsters, the Internet is something that has always been there, which means using the Web comes naturally to them.

Tech-savvy

One of the big problems adults face with their children's Internet use is that quite often children know more than they do about the online world. This means monitoring your child's Internet use can be difficult, especially as so much online activity is conducted on smartphones and other mobile devices these days. However, it is important to understand the risks children could be exposed to and what you can do to minimize them.

Left: In many ways, children are more Internet savvy than their parents.

The World Wide Wild West

The Internet offers plenty of educational and social benefits for children, but it also comes with certain risks. Many adults feel very anxious about the Internet and the dangers it poses to their children, partly because of the knowledge gap between children and adults when it comes to the online world. However, while there are dangers on the Internet, understanding what they are and what you can do to minimize the risks can make you more relaxed about your children's web use.

Hot Tip

Many children feel that their parents do not understand the Internet so do not talk about their web use, which opens the door for danger. Make an effort to spend time talking about their online activities, so they feel comfortable discussing it with you.

Above: Be aware of what children are using smartphones for as well as computers.

Understanding the Web

If you are reading this book, you are already taking a step in the right direction. Understanding how the Internet works and the threats it poses can make it easier to eliminate these threats and protect your child's web use.

THE RISKS

Adults and children face similar threats online, such as malware, hackers and phishing. But the personal attacks that children risk online can be even more damaging because of their age.

The Four Cs

Particularly iniquitous risks faced by children fall into four categories.

- **Contact:** Children use all sorts of tools for communicating with others – social media, chat rooms and forums – but the people they come into contact with online can pose a risk.

- **Content:** There is a lot of material on the Internet that is not suitable for children to see.

- **Conduct:** How your children conduct themselves online can also have consequences.

- **Crime:** Criminals use the Internet, and some specifically target children.

Above: Chat rooms are places where children may encounter cyberbullies.

CYBERBULLYING

Just as adults can come under attack from online trolls, so can children. However, in many instances children can come under attack from other children, often known to them, who use emails, text messages, chat rooms and social media to intimidate and threaten, in what has come to be known as cyberbullying.

Types of Online Bullying Behaviour

Bullying can take many forms, from other children spreading rumours and gossip about your child, to threats of violence, blackmail, abusive comments and alienation. The problem with identifying if your child is being bullied is that children are very reluctant to speak about it; they may even be scared to report it in case of further attacks by the bully. In addition, your child may worry that even if they do tell you, you may not take it seriously. Indeed, what may seem like a bit of trivial name-calling may be causing your child severe anxiety, which could even lead to depression.

Consequences of Online Bullying

Generally speaking, most incidents of online bullying are minor, and early intervention can prevent it escalating. However, there have been cases where children have felt so isolated and fearful of online bullies that they have harmed themselves.

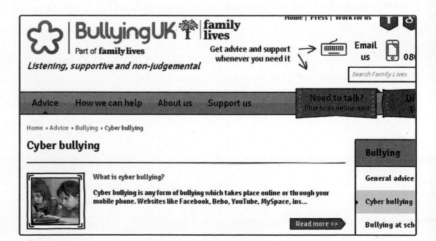

Above: Website Bullying UK (http://www.bullying.co.uk/cyberbullying/) can help you and your child deal with issues around cyberbullying.

INAPPROPRIATE CONTENT

Pornography and violent pictures and videos are not something any of us want our children exposed to. There are tools and software you can use (more on this in the next section) to guard against your children viewing such content, but there are few restrictions and checks on websites themselves to prevent minors from accessing the content.

Pornography

Adult pornography is perfectly legal, and while some websites require credit cards before people can access it, many do not. This means that anybody can click on a link or visit a web page and see pornographic material.

Illegal Material

Sexual content featuring minors (child pornography) is illegal, and viewing and possessing such material can result in a criminal prosecution, even if the people accessing it are minors themselves. Children are at risk of accessing other types of illegal material on the Internet too, such as pirated films, music and anything that promotes criminal activities.

Right: You can report illegal web content at the Internet Watch Foundation.

> ## Hot Tip
>
> If you find illegal content on the Internet, you can report it in confidence to the Internet Watch Foundation – www.iwf.org.uk/report/

Other Inappropriate Material

Not everything we would rather not have our children access is illegal or pornographic. Films, music and video games are widely available on the Internet, and some of these we may feel are unsuitable.

DAMAGED REPUTATIONS

We have already seen that things we post on the Internet can have long-lasting consequences. Images, comments and posts can stay there for ever. It is also very easy to copy and paste content from one site to another, so something that your child sends to just a few select friends could soon be available for anyone to see, even years later.

Selfies

Youngsters love sending and posting 'selfies' – photos of themselves that they have usually taken on their smartphone cameras. Selfies can be great fun, and many people take shots of themselves when out with friends or if they happen to meet a celebrity. However, there is a darker side to the selfie, and both

Above: Selfies are a popular craze; even celebrities take selfies, such as this one taken at the 2014 Oscars.

children and adults need to be aware that they should not post nude or inappropriate pictures of themselves, as they can have widespread and damaging repercussions.

> ## Hot Tip
> A photo-messaging app called Snapchat (www.snapchat.com) allows people to send pictures that disappear after a few seconds. However, it is possible for people to screen grab these images.

SEXUAL PREDATORS

Perhaps the biggest fear many parents have about their children's use of the Internet is the threat of contact with an online predator. Reports in the media about such threats may make it seem like it is all too common; thankfully, the threat of your child becoming a victim to a sexual predator is rare, but of course, it can happen.

Stranger Danger

Before the Internet, it was easy to warn children about the dangers of talking to strangers. However, in the Internet era, with social media, chat rooms, forums and text messages, it can be all too easy for strangers to make contact. Furthermore, one of the great advantages of the World Wide Web is that your children can meet and chat with children from all over the world, which can be a positive experience, but which can also pose some perils.

Left: Snapchat is a safer way for children to swap 'temporary' pictures, but while it is safer, it is still not 100 per cent safe.

Grooming

Sexual predators try to befriend and exploit children in a number of ways; these techniques are known as grooming.

- **Posing as a child**: They may pose as someone of the same age group to get close to children; often they pretend to be a child of the opposite sex interested in a relationship.

- **Personal information**: Sexual predators sometimes try to extract personal information from children, such as addresses, emails or phone numbers.

- **Bribery**: As a means of getting a child to meet up, a sexual predator may offer tickets to a pop concert, cinema or other event.

- **Blackmail**: Another known tactic is to threaten to disclose something a child has said on the Internet to make them to do something they do not want to do.

- **Intimacy**: They may ask intimate questions or send inappropriate images.

Child Exploitation and Online Protection Centre

A special criminal taskforce has been set up in the UK solely to track online sexual predators. It is called the Child Exploitation and Online Protection Centre (CEOP). If you suspect your child has been in contact with a sexual predator, you can contact CEOP at http://ceop.police.uk/

Above: CEOP police the Internet to protect children from exploitation and online grooming.

KEEPING CHILDREN SAFE

Now you know the risks faced by children on the Internet, it is time to look at the measures you can take to ensure your children are safe when they interact with the World Wide Web.

EDUCATION

Perhaps the first step in ensuring your children are safe on the Internet is to check that they know the risks. This does not mean you should frighten them, but it is worth explaining some of the basic measures you can do together to keep them safe while surfing.

- **Permanence:** It is worth reminding your children what goes online can stay online for ever.

- **Privacy:** Explain to them how privacy settings work on social media so only their friends and family can see photographs or posts.

Above: Educate your child about the risks associated with the Internet.

- **Personal information:** Reiterate the importance of being aware of how much personal or sensitive information they divulge.

- **Passwords:** Make sure they understand the importance of not sharing their passwords, except perhaps with parents.

- **Strangers:** Ensure your children know not to meet up with anybody they meet on the Internet, as they may not be who they said they were.

MONITORING WEB USE

One of the things parents find difficult is knowing where the line is between invading your child's privacy and sensible monitoring of their Internet use. Children will not appreciate you standing over their shoulder while they speak to their friends on social media, or accessing their accounts so you can read their posts, but there are other ways in which you can monitor their web use.

> **Hot Tip**
>
> Spending too much time on the Internet is not good for anybody, let alone children. Some parents set limits as to how long their children can spend online each day.

Page History

You may not feel comfortable snooping on your child's Facebook or Bebo page, but as a parent, it is sensible to ensure your children are not accessing inappropriate material, and one of the easiest ways to do this is to check their web history.

History

Clear browsing data...   Remove selected items

Today - Wednesday, October 29, 2014

☐ 12:14 PM ★ 🐦 (1) Twitter twitter.com ▾
☐ 12:12 PM 🔍 website certificate verified errors - Google
☐ 12:12 PM 📄 certificate-error.png (349×193) blog.sever
☐ 12:12 PM 🔍 website certificate cannot be verified - Goo
☐ 12:12 PM 🔍 website certificate verified errors - Google

1. On your Internet browser, select **options** (this may be represented by three horizontal lines or a gear icon).

2. Select **History**.

Above: Web history in Chrome.

3. You will be taken to a page of all the websites visited in chronological order (newest first). Click on the links if you are unsure what they are and want to check the content of the website.

RESTRICTING WEB ACCESS

In order to prevent your children from accessing inappropriate material, you may wish to restrict the type of websites they can visit. There are several ways of doing this. However, no technical solution is 100 per cent guaranteed and a determined teen may find ways around the restriction, so it is important to continue monitoring and discussing their web use with them.

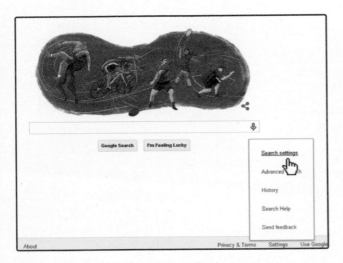

Above: Selecting Search Settings in Google.com settings.

Above: Filtering explicit content from results pages.

SAFE SEARCHING

You can prevent search engines from bringing up inappropriate content by using the 'safe search' mode.

Safe Search in Google

To set up safe search in Google, follow these steps.

1. On the Google homepage (www.google.com), click the settings link on the bottom right-hand corner.

2 Select **Search Settings**.

3. Check the **Filter explicit results** box.

4. Click **Save** at the bottom of the page.

5. You can lock safe search by setting up a Google account and clicking the **Lock Safesearch** link, which will require a password to unlock it.

Safe Search in Bing

To turn on safe search in Bing, do the following:

1. On the Bing homepage (www.bing.com) click **More** at the top of the page.

2. Select **Account** under **My Bing**.

3. Under **Safesearch** choose either **Strict** (no adult content), **Moderate** (allows some adult content but filters out hardcore pornography) or **Off** (no restrictions).

Safe Search UK

For families with young children, you may wish to use Safe Search UK as your default search engine (http://www.uk.safesearchkids.com/), which is a search engine powered by Google, but with safe search permanently on.

PARENTAL CONTROLS

As well as using safe search modes in search engines, you can use parental controls installed in your operating system or by a third-party service. Note that you have to set up these controls on every device your child has access to. (For details about setting up parental controls in mobiles and tablets, *see* page 207.)

Right: Safe Search UK is a more child-friendly search engine as it automatically filters out adult content.

> ## Hot Tip
> You can create accounts on Google for different members of your family, allowing you to restrict the content your children can access but allowing adults unrestricted access.

Safe Search UK:

powered by Google

[Google Custom Search]

[SafeSearch UK]

Safe Search UK delivers safe results from google.co.uk, powered by Google. Using this website filters explicit material for kids online in the UK.

Safe Search is automatically activated for all search terms.

Advertising Campaign Monitor: **Download AVG FREE ANTIVIRUS 2**
24/7 advertising campaign monitoring.   AVG 2014 is a free Antivirus that
web site down? Advertise off! When your   provides real-time protection and in-

WINDOWS FAMILY SAFETY

Windows has a parental control feature called Family Safety. While it comes installed as standard on Windows 8 machines, for older operating systems (from XP onwards), you have to download and install the Windows Essential package (available free from http://windows.microsoft.com/en-gb/windows-live/essentials).

Using Family Safety

Family Safety has several features you can use to protect your children when using the Internet.

- **Time restrictions:** Lets you limit the amount of time your child can use the PC or Internet.

- **Website access:** Limits the type of websites your child can visit.

- **Applications and games:** Limits the programs and games your child can use.

- **Time of day:** Lets you set times during which they can use the computer.

Above: You sign into Family Safety at https://familysafety.live.com, using your Microsoft Live log-in details.

Setting Up Family Safety

1. Once you have installed Family Safety, you have to create a Windows Live account (**https://login.live.com**) and then set up a user account for each child.

2. Select Windows Live Family Safety from your list of programs in the **Start** menu.

3. Set yourself as an 'administrator' and each child as a 'user' by selecting **Create a new Windows account**.

Restricting Internet Use with Family Safety

1. To make changes to web access, visit **https.familysafety.live.com**. Click **Edit settings** next to the account you want to change.

2. Select **Web filtering lists**. You can enter a website address and choose whether to **Allow** or **Block** it. Click **Save** when you have finished.

3. Click the **Time Limits** to specify what time of the day the PC can or cannot be used.

4. To monitor activity, click **View activity report** next to the account you wish to monitor, and you will see which sites your child has attempted to access.

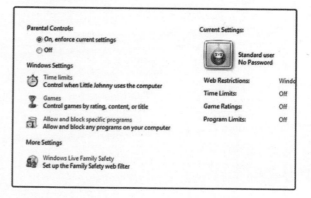

Web filtering

- ⦿ Turn on web filtering
- ⦾ Turn off web filtering

Allow list only
Only allows websites that a parent has added to the Allow list.

Child-friendly
Also allows websites in the child-friendly category. Blocks adult sites.

General interest
Also allows websites that are of general interest. Still blocks adult sites.

Online communication (basic)
Also allows social networking, web chat, and web mail. Still blocks adult sites.

Warn on adult
Allows all websites but warns when the sites contain suspected adult content.

Above: Web filtering on Windows Family Safety.

Parental Controls:
- ⦿ On, enforce current settings
- ⦾ Off

Windows Settings

Time limits
Control when Little Johnny uses the computer

Games
Control games by rating, content, or title

Allow and block specific programs
Allow and block any programs on your computer

More Settings

Windows Live Family Safety
Set up the Family Safety web filter

Current Settings:

Standard user
No Password

Web Restrictions: Windo

Time Limits: Off

Game Ratings: Off

Program Limits: Off

Above: Time limits and other options on Windows Family Safety.

PARENTAL CONTROLS OS X

Mac OS X machines have a parental control system installed in the operating system that allows you to limit web use, place time controls on computer use, as well as restrict applications and games.

Hot Tip

If your child attempts to visit a blocked site, Windows Family Safety sends you a message by email or MSN Messenger and lets you request or deny permission for access.

Setting Up OS X Parental Controls

1.   Click the Apple menu (top left) and select **System Preferences**.

Above: Creating a new account in OS X.

Above: Activating and opening Parental Controls.

2.   Select **Accounts**. Add a new account for each user by clicking the **+** sign (lower left). Keep each account **Standard** and fill out the rest of the fields before hitting **Create Account**.

3.   Select the account you want to add parental controls to and check the **Enable parental controls** box.

4.   Click on **Open Parental Controls**.

Adjusting OS X Parental Controls

When you have opened up the parental controls, you will see a number of options that will allow you to set various restrictions.

⊙   **Apps:** Here you can limit the types of applications that your child has access to as well as set an age restriction for the app store.

⊙   **Web**: Allows you to block or allow certain websites. You can also let the system limit access to adult content, although this is not 100 per cent guaranteed.

⊙   **Limits:** You can set limits to what your child can access as well as various time limits.

THIRD-PARTY SOFTWARE

There is also a range of third-party software solutions, which let you limit your child's web use.

○ **PC moderator (http://www.pcmoderator.com/):** Hardware devices that turn off your monitor after a set time limit.

○ **Safe eyes (http://www.internetsafety.com/):** A web-based system that lets you control your entire family's web use. Available for both Windows and Mac machines.

○ **ContentProtect (http://www.contentwatch.com/):** A flexible content-filtering system but more aimed at corporate web filtering. However, it is highly effective at blocking adult content from family machines.

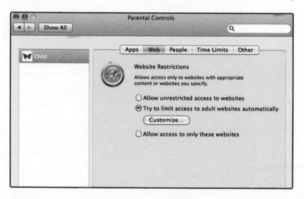

Above: The various options in OS X parental controls.

○ **iShield (http://ishield.ph/):** Prevents children from accessing pornographic sites whether accidentally or deliberately. It uses image-recognition software to identify nudity and sexual acts.

○ **KuruPira webfilter (http://www.kurupira.net/en/):** A free and easy-to-use software platform that lets you block web access, set time limits and monitor web use.

Above: Safe Eyes is a third-party parental control program.

ANTIVIRUS, FIREWALLS AND OTHER PROTECTION

ANTIVIRUS SOFTWARE

The Internet is full of malware threats, and the easiest way to protect your computer is to ensure you have some form of antivirus software. However, before you can go looking for antivirus software, you need to understand the different sorts of features they offer and the protection they provide.

MALWARE PROTECTION

The term antivirus is a bit of a misnomer, because some antivirus software not only provides virus protection but also guards you against other malware threats, such as Trojan horses, spyware and adware. However, not all antivirus software is the same and the choice can sometimes be overwhelming.

Help protect your PC

Security essentials

Security Center helps you manage your Windows security settings. To help protect your computer, make sure the three security essentials are marked ON. If the settings are not ON, follow the recommendations. To return to the Security Center later, open Control Panel.
What's new in Windows to help protect my computer?

Firewall	ON ⩔
Automatic Updates	ON ⩔
Virus Protection	ON ⩓

AVG AntiVirus Free Edition 2014 reports that it is up to date and virus scanning is on. Antivirus software helps protect your computer against viruses and other security threats. How does antivirus software help protect my computer?

Manage security settings for:

Internet Options   Automatic Updates   Windows Firewall

Above: All computers need some form of antivirus protection to guard against malware threats.

A Variety of Solutions

Antivirus software varies in price, complexity and protection, so knowing what the best solution is for you can be difficult. Sometimes, on a machine with a lot of inbuilt protection, only a basic package is necessary, while on more basic machines, you may require a more sophisticated software solution. However, before we look at the various choices on the market, it is worth examining how antivirus software works.

BASIC FUNCTIONS

While the vast majority of malware is spread via the Internet, this is not the only source. Email attachments, programs and files, USB memory sticks and even CDs and DVDs can harbour malware. For this reason, antivirus software has to be able to identify malware for a number of different locations, and it does this in two ways.

- **Virus shield**: The virus shield acts like a gatekeeper, examining all the files you download, whether from the Internet, an email attachment or another source, looking for any malware.

- **Virus scan**: There is little point in checking new files for malware if your system is already infected, which is why antivirus software can also scan your hard drives and removable media for threats.

Above: Antivirus software can scan your computer for threats.

Virus Database

One of the ways antivirus software identifies threats is by the use of a virus database. Antivirus software developers compile these databases, and when their software comes across a piece of code similar to something on the virus database, it is flagged as a possible threat. However, virus databases do have limitations.

Hot Tip

When you install antivirus software for the first time, make sure you do a thorough scan of your hard drive. It may take some time but it is the only way to be sure your machine is not already infected.

- **Polymorphic viruses**: Some viruses can modify themselves so may no longer resemble an existing threat on the database.

- **Update**: If a virus has yet to be identified, or the antivirus software has not updated its database to include the latest threats, some malware may get through.

Heuristic Scanning

Because of the above limitations, some antivirus software can also identify threats by monitoring the behaviour of files and programs on a computer. If it spots something unusual, such as program trying to overwrite another program, it flags it up as a possible threat, allowing you to take action. This is known as heuristic scanning.

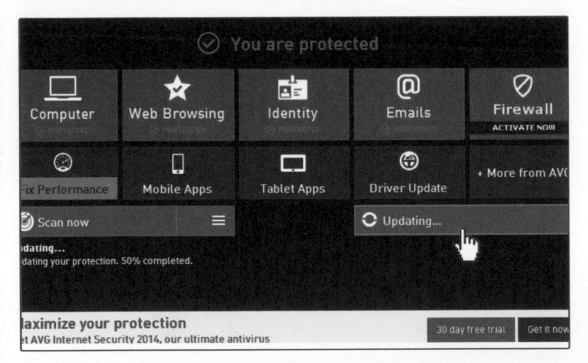

Above: It is important to keep your antivirus software updated.

DEALING WITH THREATS

When antivirus software comes across a threat, it can deal with it in several ways. Your antivirus programs may offer you the choice of what to do with a threat or it may take the action it thinks most appropriate, which includes:

- **Cleaning**: If your antivirus software identifies something that it is certain is a threat, it may erase it completely.

- **Quarantine**: If your antivirus software is unsure that something is a threat, it may quarantine it, allowing you to investigate it later. You can release a file from quarantine at any time.

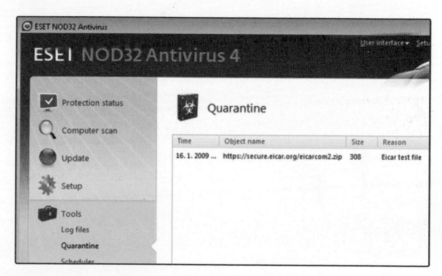

Above: If your antivirus software spots a potential threat, it may isolate it by placing it in quarantine.

- **Ignore**: If your antivirus spots something that could be a threat but is dormant, it may decide to ignore the threat and only take action if the suspicious item does something to threaten the system.

> ## Hot Tip
> When a file is quarantined, it can no longer carry out its programmed behaviour or infect another file. If you are unsure whether a file is malware or not, quarantine it, and see what effect it has on your computer.

OPERATING ENVIRONMENT

Traditionally, antivirus software has been considered only necessary for Windows machines. This was because Mac computers, Linux machines and smartphones used to be more secure than Windows-based machines as fewer people created viruses for these platforms. However, times are changing and this is no longer the case.

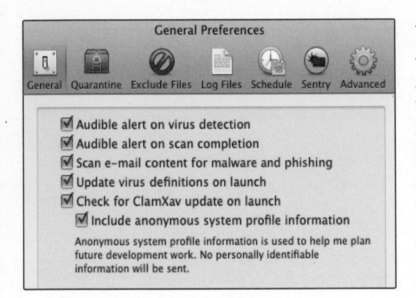

Above: Even Mac computers need antivirus software.

Antivirus Software For Mac

The increase in people using Apple products has made them a tempting target for hackers and malicious coders. This has made antivirus software just as crucial for users of Apple devices as it is for Windows machines. Not only do desktop computers and laptops require protection, but smartphones and tablets too.

Windows 8

Before the release of the latest Microsoft operating system, Windows users needed separate antivirus software. Although Windows 8 now includes its own antivirus system, known as Windows Defender many users prefer to use a third-party program, as they feel they are more effective at protecting against threats.

Hot Tip

We will look at smartphone and tablet antivirus and security software in more detail from page 201.

CHOOSING YOUR ANTIVIRUS SOLUTION

With such an array of choices of antivirus software on the market, it can be difficult to decide what solution is best for you. To help you decide, we will explore the different options and see what types of protection are available.

NOT ALL ANTIVIRUS SOFTWARE IS THE SAME

A common misconception about Internet security is that it does not matter what sort of antivirus protection you have on your computer, as long as you have some. This has led to a tendency for people to opt for free or cheap solutions, believing they offer the same protection as the more expensive software packages. However, this is not the case. Different antivirus software packages come with a wide variety of options and functions, and the solution that best suits your needs will depend on your Internet use and the risks you expose yourself to.

Right: Free antivirus software, such as AVG, offers basic levels of protection, but you may need more depending on your computer use.

Hot Tip

Some antivirus software packages are sold on a subscription basis, so make sure you understand what the total monthly and yearly costs will be before you commit.

Log in to AVG MyAcc

AVG
PC   Mac   Mobile   Tablet   **Business**

Get our essential award-wir
free protection

for your mobi

AVG AntiVirus FRE
Free Download

| Our best protection | Free Mobile Protection | Slow PC? | AVG Zen™ |
| AVG Internet Security 2014 | The #1 downloaded antivirus on | Get it back in the fast lane | The future is com |

FUNCTIONALITY

Antivirus software can contain all sorts of different features and functions. Some software, such as free packages, includes just basic functionality, while other programs include sophisticated features.

Basic Functions

At the very least, any antivirus software needs to offer the following functions:

- **Scanning**: So you can scan your files and folders to spot potential infection.

- **Shield**: Some real-time scanning is crucial for spotting threats before they can infect your files and folders.

- **Updates**: An obsolete antivirus program will be useless at spotting recent threats and the latest viruses, so ensure your program can be regularly updated.

Additional Functions

Depending on your computer usage and existing security measures, you may want other functions beyond the basics.

- **Email scanning**: Not all antivirus packages scan emails and attachments.

- **Heuristic scanning**: Some antivirus solutions only rely on databases; heuristic scanning enables your software to spot unknown and newer threats by monitoring the behaviour of files.

- **Antispyware**: Basic packages do not always protect against spyware threats.

- **Adware protection**: Not all antivirus software offers adware protection.

YOUR NEEDS

What you use your computer for can determine the types of threats you will be exposed to and the type of antivirus functionality you may need.

- **Internet surfers**: If you spend a lot of time surfing the Internet, you will need to ensure your antivirus protects you from adware, spyware and other threats you may face on the Web.

- **Gamers**: Some antivirus software can prevent games from accessing the Internet, so you need to ensure you adopt a solution that does not impinge on your online gaming.

- **Media**: If you download a lot of films, music and other files, you will want something that can spot threats as soon as they arrive on your computer.

Above: The paid-for version of AVG offers more features and functionality.

Hot Tip

Some antivirus software solutions come with a free trial. Make sure you take advantage so you can try it out and ensure you are choosing the right solution for your needs.

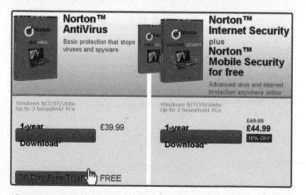

Above: Most antivirus developers offer a 30-day free trial.

○ **Office**: If you use your computer mainly for office work, you will want to ensure you have an email scanner for sending and receiving attachments.

○ **Children**: Those with a family may want a package with parental controls.

Platform

Another factor you need to take into account when choosing your antivirus software is the machine you are using and the operating system you are running. Some antivirus software requires a lot of system resources to run, which may make it unsuitable for some older machines as it may slow things down and reduce performance; some solutions do not support older operating systems (they may install but no longer update). In addition, some antivirus software performs better on certain operating systems and computers than on others.

Detection Rates

Developers of antivirus software vary in their efficiency too. Some companies such as Symantec and McAfee have been developing antivirus solutions for decades and have the experience to provide high-level detection rates, but some companies are quite new to antivirus software, so their systems may not be as effective.

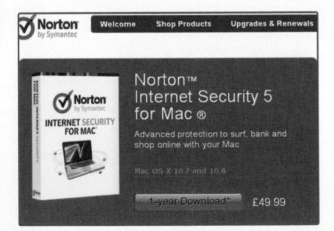

Cost

As with many other things, when looking at antivirus software, you get what you pay for, and some of the best solutions tend to be the most expensive. However, work within your budget, as the last thing you need is to install a package then find you cannot afford the subscription, eventually leaving you unprotected.

Above: Not all antivirus developers make versions for Macs or tablets.

Shortcomings

There are a few other things to consider when choosing antivirus software.

○ **Learning curve:** Some software solutions can be incredibly complicated in all but their basic functions, so choose something that you find user-friendly.

○ **System resources:** Ensure your computer is able to cope with the demands of the antivirus software; the last thing you want is your screen freezing or your machine slowing down when your antivirus is updating or scanning.

○ **Updates:** Make sure the system you choose has frequent and regular updates in order to keep you protected from the latest threats.

○ **Compatibility:** Antivirus software may prevent some innocent programs from working or accessing the Internet. Make sure the antivirus you choose is compatible with your current software.

○ **Support:** Choose antivirus software that comes with technical support so you can speak to a technician if

Hot Tip

When choosing antivirus software, do your research. Go online and read reviews of antivirus solutions, and go on forums such as http://www.antivirusforum.net/forum.php to see what people are saying about the different software.

Above: You can get all sorts of help and advice on antivirus forums that can help you choose the right software for you.

THE SOLUTIONS

It is time to look at some of the antivirus solutions available. In this section, we will explore some of the main software on the market, examine their advantages and disadvantages, costs, and how effective they are at dealing with threats.

THE BIG PLAYERS

When it comes to antivirus, two names have dominated the market for years – McAfee and Symantec. As Internet technology advances and people realize the importance of Internet security, this is now changing and the antivirus market is becoming increasingly crowded as more companies are developing software to meet the demand. However, Symantec, which produces Norton Antivirus, and McAfee remain two of the largest companies.

McAFEE

(HTTP://WWW.MCAFEESTORE.COM/)

Founded in 1987 by British-American computer programmer John McAfee, the company is now owned by Intel Corporation. McAfee produce new versions of their antivirus solutions each year and the products are licensed for 12 months, meaning you have to repay your subscription to continue using them. You are also restricted to the number of devices you can run the software on.

Did You Know?

All costs listed are correct at the time of writing this book and represent the actual UK and USA costs, not the pound to dollar conversion. However, many antivirus developers run regular half-price promotions.

Cost

McAfee produce various antivirus packages for PC, Mac, smartphone and tablet computers. These packages vary from £49.99/$49.99 for their basic *Antivirus Plus* package to £79.99/$99.99 for their *All Access Suite*, which provides protection for multiple devices, including tablets, smartphones, PCs and Macs.

Above: McAfee have been producing antivirus software for over 20 years.

Features

Even the basic McAfee's antivirus package contains all the features you require in antivirus software, including phishing protection, virus and spyware protection, and web and email scanning, as well as a built-in firewall. McAfee is easy to use, with a simple interface and plenty of help options available.

Reviews

Various third-party tests have suggested that while McAfee products are good at spotting threats, they are not as effective as other solutions at removing them. *Computer Shopper Magazine* gave their Total Protection package 2.5 out of 5 stars, while *CNET* gave the same product a rating of 3.5 out of 5 stars.

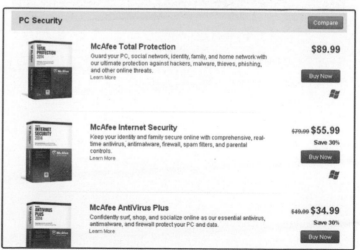

Above: McAfee produce numerous different packages that vary in price.

NORTON/SYMANTEC (HTTP://NORTON.COM/)

Founded in 1982, Symantec produced their first antivirus solution in 1989. Under the brand name Norton, the company releases new antivirus software all the time and, unlike McAfee, they no longer identify newer versions with a year-of-version number, enabling them to install updates to current versions without you having to wait for the latest product.

Cost

Prices for Norton antivirus products range from £39.99/$49.99 a year for their basic package to £69.99/$89.99 for their 360 Multi Device package (licensed for up to three devices).

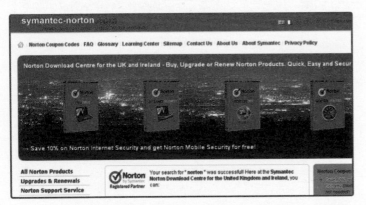

Above: Symantec's Norton offers some of the best antivirus packages on the market.

Features

Symantec's basic Norton AntiVirus provides basic virus protection, the detection and removal of spyware, the prevention of Internet worms and free technical support, while their advanced packages also include features such as parental controls and hacker protection.

Reviews

Older Symantec products used to be criticized for using too many system resources and slowing machines down, but these problems have been addressed in the latest versions, which have been recognized in recent years by both *PCMag* and *PC World* as being among the best on the market.

OTHER PLAYERS

Symantec and McAfee no longer have the dominance they once had in the antivirus market. New antivirus developers are emerging all the time, and while it is impossible to list every software manufacturer, here are some of the most popular and well-regarded solutions available.

KASPERSKY (HTTP://WWW.KASPERSKY.COM/)

Russian-based Kaspersky Lab was founded in 1997, and has built up a solid reputation for producing highly effective antivirus solutions.

Cost

The personal computing packages range from £29.99/ $33.00 for their basic package on a single device to £49.99/$66.00 for their Multi-Device and Pure, which are enhanced antivirus systems for use on up to three devices.

Features

Along with basic features such as virus scanning, Kaspersky also has an intelligent firewall system built into their software, which does not block things such as online games. They also include anti-phishing, spam filters and parental control in most packages.

Reviews

Most independent testers have awarded Kaspersky products very high scores for spotting and eliminating threats, with *PC World* awarding 4.5 out of 5 stars and *PC Mag* 4 out of 5 stars, with the only criticism being that it can be quite demanding on system resources.

Right: Kaspersky are fairly new to the antivirus market but have built a solid reputation.

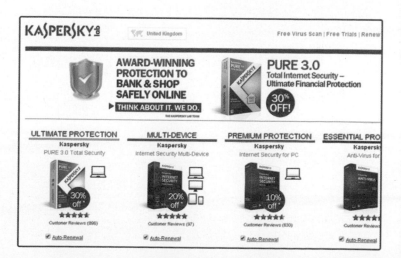

TREND MICRO

(HTTP://WWW.TRENDMICRO.COM/)

Trend Micro Internet Security (known as PC-cillin in Australia and Virus Buster in Japan) is the company's latest foray in antivirus software. Trend Micro produces antivirus software for PC, Mac and smartphone and tablet computers.

Cost

Varying in price from £39.95/$39.95 for basic protection and £79.95/$99.95 for their Titanium Maximum Security package, Trend Micro produces neither the cheapest solution on the market nor the most expensive.

Above: Trend Micro's Titanium Maximum Security can protect PCs, Macs and smartphones.

Features

With malicious URL blocking, anti-phishing and anti-spam protection, Trend Micro produces a very good all round antivirus solution, tailored for heavy Internet users.

Reviews

PC Mag awarded Trend Micro 4 out of 5 stars for their Titanium Antivirus Plus, with the major criticism being that the system can be over-zealous, often blocking non-threats.

QUICK HEAL

(HTTP://WWW.QUICKHEAL.COM/)

Indian-based Quick Heal has been producing antivirus software since the mid-1990s, but has come to prominence in recent years due to its unique Advanced Machine Learning capabilities, making it one of the most effective antivirus solutions on the market for spotting threats.

Hot Tip

For those wanting extreme protection against online threats, it is possible to run more than one antivirus solution at once, although not all software is compatible with one another.

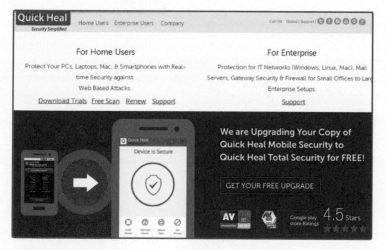

Above: Quick Heal has plenty of low-cost solutions.

Cost

Quick Heal is sold via a US website, but UK customers can buy and download any of their antivirus solutions, which vary from $30 to $74 a year. They also have low-cost smartphone and tablet solutions, starting at $7 a year!

Features

The biggest benefit offered by Quick Heal is not only its effectiveness at spotting threats, but it is also very light on system resources, making it quick and efficient.

Reviews

Scored 98.29 points out of 100 in independent tests in 2010 when it was awarded PC Security Labs certification.

ESET

Slovak-based ESET produced their first antivirus system called NOD32 back in 1987. Based on their original NOD32 system, ESET Smart Suite is aimed at Internet users and is a simple-to-use but fairly basic antivirus package.

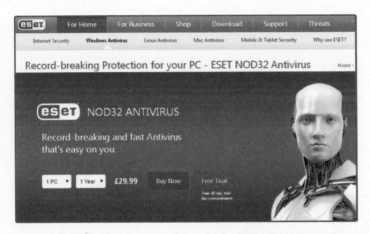

Above: ESET's NOD32 was developed in the 1980s.

Cost

ESET produce Smart Suite, which ranges from £39.99/$59.99 for one PC per year, to £69.99/$89.99 for five licences, and its basic NOD32 antivirus software (£29.99/$39.99).

Features

This is a very basic system with good malware protection but with only rudimentary firewall and parental control.

Reviews

Many people like Smart Suite for its simplicity, although others have criticized it for its inability to deal with threats as effectively as comparable systems. *PC Mag* awarded the latest version of Smart Suite 2.5 out *of 5*.

BIT DEFENDER

Launched in 2001 by Romanian-based Softwin, Bit Defender is the relatively new kid on the block when it comes to antivirus software, but has gained a solid reputation for protection against online threats.

Cost

Bit Defender comes in three basic packages: Antivirus Plus (£39.95/$49.95), Internet Security (£49.95/$69.95) and Total Security (£59.95/$79.95).

Features

Even Bit Defender's basic package, Anti Virus Plus, is crammed full of features that you have to pay for on comparable software. These include phishing protection, ID-theft monitoring, password management, private data, financial transaction protection and a Facebook profile scanner, while the more advanced packages have remote management and multi-device parental control.

Reviews

Most independent tests scored Bit Defender well above average and their Anti Virus Plus scored 4.5 out of 5 in *PC Mag*.

Left: Bit Defender is award-winning antivirus software.

MICROSOFT SECURITY ESSENTIALS

The latest version of Microsoft Windows, Windows 8, comes with its own antivirus program installed called Windows Defender. For older versions of Windows, Microsoft Security Essentials can be downloaded at: http://windows.microsoft.com/en-GB/windows/security-essentials-download/ although support for Windows XP has now ended.

Cost

While it is only available for users of Windows PCs running Windows Vista with Service Pack 1 or Service Pack 2, Windows 7 and Windows 8, it is completely free of charge for home users and for small businesses (on up to 10 devices). However, it may well be free, but is it in any good?

Hot Tip

PC Mag (http://pcmag.com) **reviews and tests nearly all antivirus software produced, so they are a good resource for discovering the pros and cons of available solutions.**

Features

Microsoft Security Essentials is quite a small file (24 MB), but it contains all the basic antivirus functions of paid-for software, such as malware protection, real-time scanning and monitoring, as well as a System Restore facility. It is also easy to use and runs in tandem with Windows Firewall.

Reviews

Many independent testers found that while Microsoft Security Essentials does an adequate job protecting and getting rid of online

Above: A version of Windows Essentials, called Windows Defender is already installed on Windows 8 machines.

threats, it does not offer the same level of protection as some of the paid-for solutions. However, it still scored 3 out of 5 in *PC Mag*, better than some of the most costly solutions.

OTHER FREE PROGRAMS

Microsoft Security Essentials is not the only free antivirus protection available. Other developers also have free versions available. Some of these are basic packages that can be upgraded with additional features at a cost, while others produce free home versions but charge for business users, hoping that the positive experience of personal users encourages businesses to buy.

○ **AVG (http://www.avg.com/):**
By far the most popular free antivirus software available, users are offered basic malware protection, link protection and file shredding but can pay to upgrade for anti-spam, an online shield and a firewall.

○ **Avast (http://www.avast.com/):**
Also offers upgrades to improve on the basic malware protection of the free version with financial transaction protection, a firewall and anti-spam protection.

Hot Tip
You can test several antivirus solutions yourself by installing trial versions and free versions and getting them to scan your machine. You may find some solutions identify threats on your computer that others have missed.

RIGHT: AVG is the most popular free antivirus software available.

- **Avira (http://www.avira.com/):** Claims to detect 99.99% of malware. Avira also comes with a browser toolbar that has an anti-phishing tool and social media protection.

- **Panda Cloud (http://www.cloudantivirus.com/):** A free version of a commercial product that contains basic protection in a lightweight package.

BUSINESS USERS

Some antivirus software developers permit their free or home software to be used by small and medium-sized businesses. This may make financial sense as you will get basic level of protection that could be enough to meet your needs. However, larger organizations with hundreds of devices to protect, or those companies with a need for more enhanced security, should consider opting for a business package from one of the main antivirus developers.

Business Packages

With a business package, you can deploy the antivirus software over your network, rather than having to install the software individually on each machine. A licence for business software is often over two years (as opposed to one for home use) and while it is limited to set number of machines – so the more machines you need to protect the more licences you will need to buy – the cost per machine can often work out to be cheaper than using a home licence.

Left: Most antivirus developers produce business versions of their software.

USING ANTIVIRUS SOFTWARE

Once you have installed antivirus software on your computer, you will need to learn how to use it. Fortunately, most of the basic functions of antivirus software are easy to get to grips with, no matter which program you have opted for.

INSTALLATION

Antivirus software is installed in much the same way as any other software program.

1. Whether your software is on a disk or you have downloaded it, click the setup icon (on a Mac click the installer).

2. Follow the steps as indicated by the installer, for example click run when asked if you want to run the file, and choose a location where you want your software installed.

3. You may have to enter a registration key to activate your software.

4. Once installed, most antivirus software programs will run automatically but if yours does not, click on the program icon in either your program menu or in the antivirus folder.

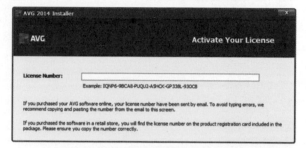

Above: You may be asked to enter a registration key; this will be on the box or will be sent to you by email.

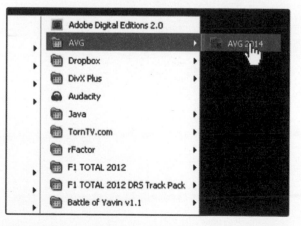

Above: Clicking the AVG icon in the program's menu.

Control Panel

When your antivirus software is installed on your computer, you will see a small icon in the lower right-hand corner of your Windows taskbar (on a Mac, this may be in the top right, or you may have to open up **System Preferences)**. When you double click this icon, it will bring up the antivirus control panel. Control panels for antivirus software normally include the different functions.

Above: Norton control panel.

Above: McAfee control panel.

- **Computer:** This will tell you if your computer is protected. If you have not run an initial scan, this will show that action is required. There will normally be a **Fix** or **Scan Now** button.

- **Internet:** Where you will find your browser protection tools.

- **Emails:** Where you can run email scans.

- **Firewall:** Where you can turn on and control your antivirus firewall (if included).

- **Others:** You may have sections for identity protection, parental controls and other additional features included in your antivirus software.

- **Updates:** Where you can update your antivirus software.

SCANNING

When your antivirus software is installed it will most likely ask you if you want to run an initial scan. This is important as it will check your hard drive for any existing threats and remove them. If you are not prompted to run an initial scan, go into the control panel of your antivirus software. You will probably find a simple interface, with a section labelled **Scanning**; go into this and run a full scan.

Hot Tip

Most antivirus software will allow you to schedule when you want updates. Make sure you update it daily, perhaps when you first boot up your machine. That way, you will always be protected from the most recent threats.

Update

Before your antivirus software can run a full scan it may need to update its virus database so it can spot recent threats. This may take several minutes. Most software will do this automatically, but it may prompt you with a window asking for your permission to update; just click yes.

Above: Running a scan in AVG.

SETTING UP YOUR PROTECTION

When installed, antivirus software normally starts in a default mode, which ensures your system is secure from the outset. However, this default mode may not provide you with all the features you require in operation, or it may be too strict, slowing the performance of your machine down as it runs unnecessary scans. You can adjust the various different settings to ensure you are getting the most out of your antivirus software.

Shield

Your antivirus shield is normally in the **Computer** protection settings. The purpose of the shield is to stop threats entering your computer, but the way it does this can be adjusted using a settings menu (you may have to double click the **Computer** tab to see the settings menu or click a **settings** link).

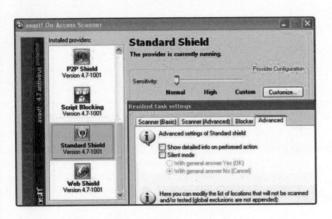

Above: Adjusting shield settings in Avast.

○ **Permission:** Your antivirus software may remove threats automatically or you can set it to ask your permission first.

○ **Reporting:** The software may be able to report potentially unwanted programs or possible threats that are not yet on its database.

○ **Heuristics:** Enabling heuristics lets your antivirus software look for suspicious behaviour or code.

Scans

There are all sorts of options available in the scanning settings on most antivirus software.

○ **Media:** You can scan removable media plugged into your machine, your hard drive or specific files and folders.

○ **Schedules:** Allows you to schedule full or partial scans at regular intervals.

Hot Tip

A full computer scan can take some time and can slow your computer down. It is perhaps more practical to schedule a scan on a weekly basis or before you shut down your machine, rather than when you turn it on.

○ **Files**: You can set your antivirus to scan files when you open or close them.

○ **Extensions and cookies**: You can scan items in your Internet browser, such as cookies, toolbar extensions and browser helper objects (more on these on pages 235–37).

Email Scanning

Scanning emails can protect your computer from malware threats sent in attachments and can also prevent you from infecting other people's machines. You can choose whether to scan inbound or outbound emails or both.

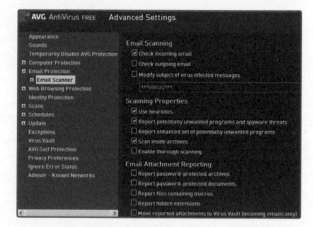

Web Browser Protection

Different antivirus solutions offer all sorts of protection when you are surfing the Internet, most of which can be adjusted in the settings.

Above: Adjusting email settings in AVG.

○ **Identity protection**: This sort of protection can guard you against phishing and spyware. However, as no system is infallible, it may block innocent emails, so you can choose whether to have it warn you or remove threats automatically.

○ **Malicious web pages**: Most antivirus software has some form of web shield that protects you from malware hidden in web pages. This can be adjusted in the settings.

○ **Toolbars and browser extensions**: Some antivirus software provides you with tools that can be installed on your browser, such as safe search bars.

○ **Search protection**: Some antivirus has software that runs on search engine pages, providing information about whether a website is trusted or may contain a threat.

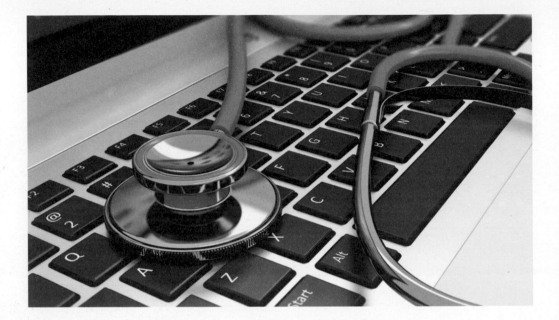

Updating

It is not only the virus database that can be updated, but most antivirus developers also release updates to the software, and it is important to regularly install these.

Quarantine

The quarantine, sometimes called a virus vault, is where your antivirus software places threats it has not removed. Once in quarantine, threats can no longer cause harm, as they are isolated from the computer. If the file is innocent and

Left: AVG safe search icons show next to Google search results.

needed by a program to run, you may find that program stops working, which is why it is a good idea to set your antivirus software to quarantine threats before deleting them.

- **Schedule**: You can schedule your antivirus software to delete threats in your quarantine after a certain time, enabling you to check whether the files are not needed. Alternatively, you can delete threats manually.

- **Size of vault**: You can also allocate how much of your hard drive you want to set aside for the virus vault.

Did You Know?

Your antivirus software will keep a record of all the threats it has found and will normally provide statistics in the settings menu, allowing you to evaluate the effectiveness of your software.

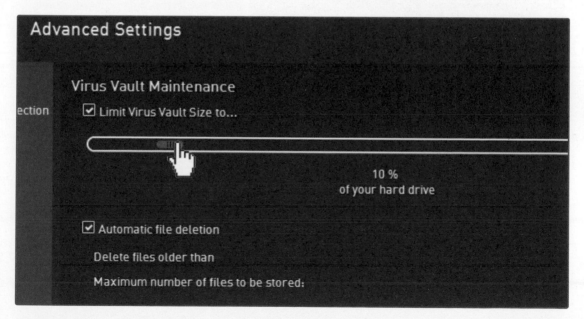

Advanced Settings

ection

Virus Vault Maintenance

☑ Limit Virus Vault Size to...

10 %
of your hard drive

☑ Automatic file deletion

Delete files older than

Maximum number of files to be stored:

Above: Adjusting the size of the virus vault in AVG.

Exceptions

If your antivirus software starts to interfere with the normal running of some programs, you can instruct the antivirus to ignore these programs from scans and threat detection. Adding exceptions is normally straightforward in most antivirus software.

Above: Exceptions menu in AVG.

Above: Browsing for a file to exclude from antivirus scans.

1. Click **Add Exception** in the exceptions settings menu.

2. Choose whether it is a file, folder or program you wish to exclude.

3. Enter or browse for the location of the item you want to exclude.

4. Select what you want to exclude the file from, such as scanning or shield protection, and click **Save**.

Reporting Back

Because antivirus software is dependent on identifying new threats and finding solutions to defend against them, your software may send a report to the developers if it finds a new threat, including data about your machine. This information is normally anonymous, and not identifiable to you, but you can usually turn this feature off if you feel uncomfortable about it.

USING FIREWALLS

Firewalls are as important as antivirus software for protecting you from threats. Most antivirus software comes with a firewall, or you may have one built into your operating system, but to ensure proper protection, you need to know how to use it properly.

WHAT IS A FIREWALL?

While your antivirus software can protect you from malware by scanning files and folders, other threats can still get through your computer, such as hackers and bots. To guard against unauthorized access, a computer or network needs a firewall. Firewalls work by filtering traffic and only letting through certain communications depending on a given set of criteria.

Did You Know?

A firewall normally acts as a one-way barrier to the Internet; while it will block traffic coming into a computer, it will allow free access for outbound traffic.

Hardware and Software

A firewall is commonly a software barrier, often installed in an operating system or with antivirus software, but you can use hardware firewalls for added protection. For more information on hardware firewalls, *see* pages 243–45.

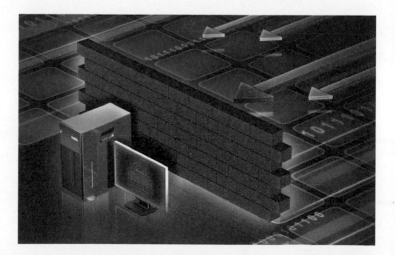

Right: Firewalls act rather more intelligently than a brick wall – filtering out dangerous traffic.

Installing Firewalls

Most antivirus software comes with a firewall, as do many operating systems. You can easily check if you have a firewall installed.

Above: Opening up the Security Center on a PC.

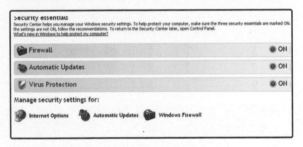

Above: Windows firewall is activated.

Above: ZoneAlarm is a popular free firewall.

1. On a Windows machine, click start and open up the **Control Panel**. On a Mac, open up the **System Preferences** from the Apple menu.

2. On a Windows machine, select the **Security Center**; on a Mac, choose **Security and Privacy**.

3. You can see if your firewall is active by the green **On** button in Windows and in the **Firewall** tab on a Mac.

Third-party Firewalls

If you do not have a firewall installed, you can buy or download free third-party firewalls. Some third-party firewalls include:

○ **ZoneAlarm (http://www.zonealarm .com/):** Has a free firewall, but also sells a compatible antivirus and security suite.

○ **Comodo (http://personalfirewall. comodo.com/):** Provides a free firewall as well as a paid-for antivirus and firewall suite called Internet Security Pro.

- **Online Armor ()**: A paid for firewall (£25.07/$40.00 per year) that is rated as one of the best on the market.

COMMON FIREWALL PROBLEMS

Most issues around firewalls are caused by the firewall blocking access to innocent programs that need to send data to your computer. Sometimes using a firewall can stop certain features of applications from working properly. In the majority of cases, these problems can be rectified by adjusting settings in your firewall to allow incoming traffic.

Exceptions

When your firewall blocks something, a box may pop up to tell you and give you the option of allowing the item through. However, it may not, in which case you have to add an exception to your firewall settings to allow data needed by the program to enter your firewall.

Hot Tip

Some programs, such as antivirus software, automatically include themselves as exceptions in your firewall settings. However, some malware can do this too, so it is worth checking to see what has been made an exception in your firewall settings.

Adding Exceptions to Windows Firewall

Adding a program as an exception to most firewalls is relatively straightforward. Here's how to add a program as an exception to Windows Firewall.

1. Open up the Windows **Security Center** and click on **Windows Firewall**.

2. In the Windows Firewall menu, click on **Exceptions**.

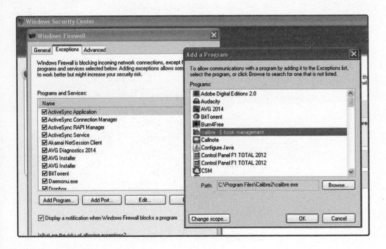

Above: Adding a program as an exception to the firewall.

3. Click **Add Programs**.

4. Select the program from the menu, or **Browse** for it on your hard drive.

5. Click **OK** to add to exceptions.

Removing an Exception

If you wish to remove a program from your list of exceptions, just select it and click **Delete**.

PORTS

When data arrives on your computer, it does so by the way of an open port. A port is simply the pathway on which data travels to your computer. Normally these pathways are blocked by the firewall, but to authorize communication, the firewall opens a port to allow access. Most software is usually programmed to send data through a specific port, but sometimes a program may not have a predetermined port number and you may need to open one or redirect the data.

Changing Port Numbers

If a program is not working properly, such as freezing or crashing, or you are receiving Windows' error messages indicating you have a software conflict or that it has blocked a port, it may be a sign you have several programs trying to use the same port and you may need to reassign the port number. However, most software will only work through certain ports, so if a user manual came with your program, look to see what ports it can work with.

1. Open up the firewall settings (here we show Windows Firewall).

2. In the **Exceptions** tab, select the program for which you need to open a new port and select **Edit** then **Change Scope**.

3. Enter the new port address.

Above: Editing a port number in Windows Firewall.

Above: Changing a port address in Windows Firewall.

Opening Ports

Sometimes your software may not be able to automatically open its own port, which means you may have to do it manually.

1.   In your firewall settings, select **Add Port**.

2.   Enter the name of the program you want to open a port for.

3.   Enter the port address (consult your software manual for suitable ports).

4.   Click **OK**.

Port Forwarding

Some hardware firewalls allow port forwarding. When you forward a port, you are redirecting the data. This is often done to speed up the performance of the data entering a network, as congested ports can slow down programs and applications. However, you cannot simply forward data to any old port, it has to be one that is compatible with your software. In addition, it is not something you should try unless you are confident you know what you are doing.

Running Multiple Firewalls

Some firewalls are compatible with each other, but generally speaking, running more than one firewall at a time can cause conflicts, which may leave your computer exposed to threats.

Turning off Your Firewall

If your firewall is causing an issue that you cannot solve, such as preventing a program from working, you can turn your firewall off using the firewall settings. However, your computer will be vulnerable to threats as long as the firewall is not on, so ensure you turn it back on again as soon as possible.

OTHER PROTECTION SOFTWARE

Antivirus and firewalls are not the only software available to guard you against online threats. Some malware can be difficult to detect and an array of additional tools and techniques is available that can help keep you secure.

JAVA AND FLASH THREATS

One of the major weaknesses on a computer when it comes to online threats is the plug-ins used by browsers that allow multimedia and interactions on websites. These are known as Flash and Java, and malicious programmers often use the inherent weaknesses in these plug-ins to attack computers.

Java

Java is a browser plug-in, used by some websites to show content. However, Java is a bit like running a virtual computer on your browser, and Java programs run on this virtual environment. This means a malware program can be written to infect Java, and it will run on any computer, PC or Mac, and your firewall and antivirus software can do little to guard against these threats.

Above: Java is used by a lot of websites for running multimedia.

Flash and Shockwave

Flash and Shockwave are plug-ins created by Adobe to run multimedia such as videos and streaming content. As with Java, malicious programs can attack these plug-ins. However,

Adobe regularly releases updates to ensure its products are secured against malware, so the best way to protect your machine from Flash and Shockwave threats is to ensure you update regularly.

> ## Hot Tip
> You can ensure you have the latest versions of Flash by downloading it directly from https://www.adobe.com/support/flashplayer/downloads.html, and the latest Shockwave at http://get.adobe.com/shockwave/

Disabling Java

While Java regularly releases updates to protect against threats, some users prefer to disable it in their Internet browser unless they are on a website they trust.

Disabling Java on a PC

1. Click the **Start** menu and scroll through your programs until you find Java.

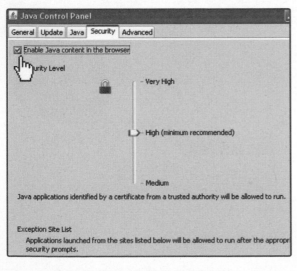

Above: Disabling Java in the Java control panel.

2. Select **Configure Java** to launch the Java Control Panel.

3. Click the **Security** tab and uncheck the **Enable Java content in the Browser**.

4. Click **Apply**.

Disabling Java on a Mac

1. Click on the Apple icon on upper left of your screen and go into **System Preferences**.

2. Click on the Java icon to launch the Java Control Panel.

3. Click the **Security** tab and uncheck the **Enable Java content in the Browser**.

4. Click **Apply**.

OTHER MALWARE TOOLS

When looking for software online, it is important you do your homework. The Internet is full of disreputable companies claiming they have legitimate products, but which in fact are selling ineffectual software packed with spyware, adware and other malicious programs. While you certainly have to be careful when downloading anti-spyware and other software from the Internet, there are still some useful tools available that can help keep you safe and clean your computer from malware threats.

Hot Tip

Beware of adware that warns you that spyware has been detected on your machine, which can be remedied by buying a certain spyware removal program. Normally, these anti-spyware tools install more malware and force you to buy more anti-spyware products further down the line.

MALWARE DETECTION TOOLS

Because no antivirus software system is perfect, you may never know when a malware threat has managed to slip past your security suite and infected your machine. Malware detection tools are not antivirus software as such, but are designed as extra levels of security to help spot threats you may not even be aware of. Often these are good for occasional scans and can be used alongside your standard antivirus software.

Malwarebytes (http://www.malwarebytes.org/)

Malwarebytes is a simple-to-use malware scanner for Windows machines that can spot and remove threats your standard software may have missed. It also includes a tool called FileASSASSIN, which can help delete locked files, caused by either malware or errors in Windows.

Super Antispyware (http://www.superantispyware.com/)

This is another free Windows malware scanner and removal tool designed to spot spyware threats. It is compatible with most major antivirus software suites, so gives great additional security for ensuring your PC is spyware free.

Above: Malwarebytes can scan for malware threats that your antivirus may have missed.

Spybot Search and Destroy (http://www.safer-networking.org/)

One of the most popular free spyware removal tools that works on any Windows machine, including older operating systems, such as XP, Windows 98 and even Windows 95.

Microsoft Safety Scanner (http://www.microsoft.com/security/scanner/en-gb/default.aspx)

A free downloadable security tool for Windows machines that provides a one-time scan and helps remove viruses, spyware and other malicious software. It works with your existing antivirus software and erases itself off your machine after 10 days.

BOTNET SCANNERS

Botnets are among the toughest online threats for antivirus software to detect. Creators of botnet malware are for ever finding weaknesses in operating systems which they then use to infect machines and recruit as botnets.

BotHunter (http://www.bothunter.net/)

Rather than relying on a database to recognize bots or analysing a computer for suspicious activity, BotHunter, which is a free program, listens to the Internet traffic through your machine for telltale signs of a botnet. When it spots a threat, it removes it and informs a database kept by its developers so that other machines can be cleaned of the same threat.

RUBotted (http://free.antivirus.com/us/rubotted/)

Another free program that works in a similar way to BotHunter, RUBotted monitors your computer for potential infection and suspicious activities associated with bots. Upon discovering a potential infection, RUBotted will identify and remove it with its HouseCall cleaner.

Right: BotHunter is one of the best tools for detecting bots on your computer.

REGISTRY CLEANERS

Your system registry is what Windows computers use to store the configuration of the operating system. The registry is often targetted as it means the malware will be installed whenever the machine boots up. While most antivirus software cam remove registry threats, there are a couple of tools you can use to remove registry entries yourself.

Hot Tip

You should never make changes to your system registry without knowing what you are doing and first backing up. Changes to your system registry can result in system crashes, requiring the reinstallation of your operating system and the loss of data.

HiJackThis (http://sourceforge.net/projects/hjt/)

This free tool scans the registry reports and registry entries that could have been altered or tampered with by spyware, malware or other malicious programs.

Above: You should only use registry cleaners such as HiJackThis if you are confident that know what you are doing.

CCleaner (https://www.piriform.com/CCLEANER)

This free program removes entries for non-existent applications in your Windows registry, fixes invalid or corrupted entries, cleans out temporary files, cookies and cached items in your browser, as well as removing temporary and log files on Windows. It even empties your recycling bin.

PC SECURITY

Because many of us keep important documents on our computers, not to mention all those passwords and usernames stored in cookies on our browsers, having a system in place to secure all this data can give you peace of mind in case your computer is lost or stolen.

Windows Bitlocker

Bitlocker is installed On Windows 7 and Windows 8 operating systems. Bitlocker isn't enabled by default, but you can activate it by checking the box in **System and Security** in the **Control Panel**. Bitlocker automatically encrypts the hard drive and protects everything from documents to saved passwords.

OTFE (http://www.portable freeware. com/?id=698)

If your operating system does not have Bitlocker, you can download OTFE for free, which encrypts files on Windows machines, including Windows Mobile, and encrypts all files before they are stored on your hard drive.

Above: Turning on Bitlocker in the Windows System and Security menu.

SMARTPHONES, TABLETS AND LAPTOPS

MOBILE SECURITY

Thanks to smartphones, tablets and Wi-Fi access points, we no longer need to be chained to our desks to access the Internet, but this freedom comes with its own security risks.

MOBILE TECHNOLOGY

One of the biggest security threats to mobile Internet technology when using such devices as smartphones, tablets and laptops, is that they make tempting targets for thieves. Furthermore, if you are on a long train journey and have been using your mobile device, it is all too easy to leave it behind, and lost or stolen smartphones, tablets and laptops can cause a security

Hot Tip

Always keep an eye on your mobile device. It does not have to be stolen for you to lose data. Hackers can slip a USB stick into an unattended device to install malware that can steal data.

Left: Accessing the Internet on the move gives us untold freedom, but this is not without its risks.

nightmare. Not only do these devices contain important files and documents, but they also may be packed full of private and personal information, including photographs, account numbers and passwords to our online accounts.

Theft Risk

Smartphones, tablets and laptops are tempting targets for thieves. Because of their size, these mobile devices are easily snatched, and thieves find them easy to sell on the black market. For this reason, it is worth taking extra care when out and about with your mobile devices.

- **Location:** Before getting out your phone or tablet, take stock of your surroundings. Note who is about and whether it is safe to get your device out.

- **Unattended:** Never leave a mobile device unattended, even for a few seconds. A phone left on a table can be easily grabbed, and never leave a mobile device in a car.

- **IMEI number:** All smartphones and tablets have a 15-digit IMEI number, usually printed under the battery. Knowing this number enables your provider to block the device if it is lost or stolen (even if it has been given a new SIM).

- **Back up:** Make sure you have a backup of all your files and photos on your phone and tablet in case the worst does happen.

Right: The IMEI number is normally situated on a barcode or next to the serial number.

iPad

64GB

Designed by Apple in California Assembled in China Model A1337
Rated 5V === 2A max. EMC 2328 Complies with the Canadian ICES-003
Class B specifications. FCC ID: BCG-E2328A and IC: 579C-E2328A
IMEI 010004000100000   Serial V00000JW0T0

PROTECTING YOUR DATA

If your tablet, smartphone or laptop is lost or stolen, you not only have the expense of replacing the device, but you also run the risk of having all your personal data fall into the wrong hands. Mobile devices are used for all sorts of things these days, from social media to online banking and email. This means that your device may contain highly sensitive data, including account numbers, usernames and passwords.

Hot Tip

Remember when coming up with a password for your phone or tablet to choose a strong one that cannot be guessed by trial and error.

Password Protection

One of the simplest ways of ensuring the data and information stored on your smartphone or tablet is secure is to take advantage of the password protection systems provided by the manufacturer. Most smartphones and tablets come with some sort of password lock, preventing any unauthorized user from gaining access to the device, and implementing it can be relatively straightforward, depending on the device in question.

Passcodes on iOS Devices

On earlier Apple tablets and phones, you can only set a four-digit passcode. However, on iOS4 and later devices, you can set a full password, providing you with added security. The lock is activated when the phone has not been used for a set length of time, and means you have to enter it to unlock the phone.

Left: If you fail to enter the correct password, most phones will lock for a minute or so.

Setting iOS Password/Passcode

1. Open the **Settings** app and choose **General**.

2. Select **Passcode Lock** and turn it on.

3. Enter your new password or passcode.

4. Back in the **General** menu you can alter the **Auto-lock** settings, the period of time after which the device will lock itself. Setting to **Immediately** means you have to enter the passcode every time you want to access the device.

Above: Turning on a passcode on an iPhone.

Did You Know?

A passcode will only prevent access to your data, it will not completely disable your phone, as it may be possible for a thief to do a 'factory reset', which will wipe your data but allow the phone to be used.

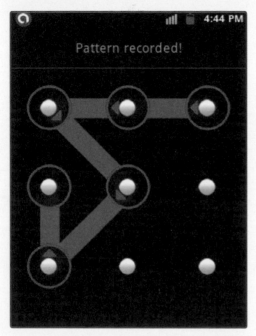

Above: Setting a lock pattern on an Android phone.

Above: If you forget your swipe lock, you can enter your Gmail account to unlock your phone.

Swipe Security on Android Devices

Most Android devices include the ability to lock a phone using a swipe pattern, a unique shape created using your finger, that will unlock the phone. As with passwords, you need to come up with something that cannot be easily guessed or cracked using trial and error. This means not using an obvious shape such as a cross or L-shape.

Setting an Android Swipe Pattern

1. Go into **Settings** and choose **Security**.

2. Select **Change Unlock Pattern** and check **Require Pattern**.

3. Swipe the pattern you want to use to unlock your phone.

Forgotten Swipe Pattern

If you forget your security pattern for your Android device, you can swipe your finger down and to the right. This will present you with the ability to enter

Did You Know?

If you fail five times to swipe the correct pattern into an Android device, the device will lock and you have to wait 30 seconds before you can try again.

your Gmail address and password (the phone or tablet has to be connected to the Internet for this to work), which, if correct and synced to the phone, will unlock it.

Additional Tablet and Smartphone Locks

Both later iOS and Android devices have other security features installed that you can use to lock/unlock your phone. To access these, you need to visit the security menu in your device's settings.

○ **Face unlock:** Some tablets and smartphones allow the use of facial recognition software that ensures only your face can unlock the device.

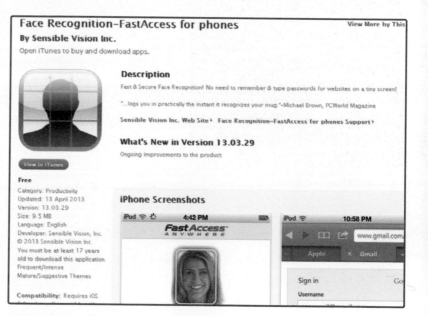

○ **Signature:** Some devices, such as the Galaxy Note tablet, let you lock/unlock the device using your written signature.

Above: You can install facial recognition software on later iPhones.

○ **Passwords and PIN:** Some Android devices, such as 2.2 Froyo, permit the use of passcodes and passwords.

○ **SIM card PIN:** To prevent someone removing your SIM card and using it in another phone, you can set a PIN lock on some smartphones.

SETTINGS

system applica

ringtones+sounds

theme

email+accounts

internet sharing

lock screen

WiFi

Above: Lock-screen settings on a Windows phone.

Keylock on Windows Phones and Tablets

Windows phones and tablets utilize either a version of the Windows Mobile operating system or Windows 8. Windows 8 permits the use of password locking as with normal PCs and laptops (*see* **Securing a Laptop** on page 190), while some Windows phones, such as those using Windows Phone 7, allow you to set a lock-screen password.

1. On your application list, select **Settings**.

2. Press **Lock Screen** and turn on the **Password** option (if not already on).

3. You will be prompted to enter a new password twice. After this, press **Done** to save your changes.

Other Devices

Of course, Android, iOS and Windows are not the only operating systems available for smartphones and tablets. It is impossible to cover the security features for all devices and operating systems in this book, but most devices will have some form of key-lock security, which you can set by going into your security settings.

REMOTE WIPE

As its name suggests, Remote Wipe is a function that enables you to wipe the contents of your phone remotely, so if your device is stolen, you can be assured nobody will be able to access your files or online accounts. It works by restoring your device to the factory settings, erasing everything in the process, including numbers, files, photos, saved passwords and browser history.

Remote Wipe on iOS Devices

Organizing remote wipe on Apple devices is fairly simple, but you need to set up a few things first.

- **iCloud:** You need to set up an iCloud account so you can access Apple's online services.

- **iOS 4.2 and earlier:** For older Apple devices, you need to enable **Push** and **Find My iPhone** in the **Settings** app under **Mail, Contacts, Calendars**.

Wiping Your iOS Device

1. Log into iCloud and click the **Account** button at the top of the screen.

2. Select the **Find My iPhone, iPad, iPod Touch or Mac** option once the page loads.

3. Select **All Devices** and choose the device you want to erase.

4. In the device's information window, select **Erase**.

Above: You can remote wipe an iPhone using the iCloud service.

Above: Finding your iPhone in iCloud.

Did You Know?

If your phone or iPad is offline, it will erase as soon as it goes online again. You should receive a notification by email when it is erased, but for some older models, this can take as long as two hours.

Google

One account. All of Google.

Sign in to continue to Gmail

Email

Password

Sign in

☑ Stay signed in   Need help?

Create an account

Above: You need to sync a Gmail account to your phone to use remote wipe.

Above: Android Device Manager.

Remote Wipe on Android Devices

Remote wipe on an Android device is called **Lock & Erase** but it is a lot more complicated to set up, and you need to have several things in place before you can utilize it.

- **Android 2.2**: You can only set up remote wipe on devices running Android 2.2 or later.

- **Google Account**: Before you can set up remote wipe on an Android device, you need to have a Google account, which is synchronized with your device.

- **Remote access**: The device needs to be set up for remote access.

Setting Android Remote Access and Lock & Erase

In order to set up remote wipe on an Android device, you first have to enable remote access.

1. Set up your Google account on your device.

2. On a separate computer, log into your Google account, and then go to **www. google.com/android/devicemanager/**

3. Click on the **Accept** button.

4. The page should display your device name. Click on **Setup Lock & Erase** and click on the **Send** button to send a message to your Android device, confirming remote lock and reset.

Android Device Manager

GT-S5830i

Location unavailable
Last online July 25, 2014

Ring | Lock | Erase

Glasgow

North

United Kingdom

Isle of Man

Liverpool   Sheffield

Ireland

5. On your Android device, confirm access. You will then be taken to the activation page, where you will be required to tap on the **Activate** button to set up **Lock & Erase**.

Above: Once you have allowed access on your phone, you will be able to lock or erase remotely.

6. Check the box for **Remote locate this device** and **Allow remote lock and factory reset**. Tap on the check box for both options to enable remote locking and wiping of your device.

7. You will now be able to log into the Android Device Manager on any computer, where you will see the **Lock** and **Erase** options, which will allow you to remotely lock or erase your device.

Hot Tip
You can get remote wipe apps for Android phones. See the section on Other Security Measures on page 192 for more information.

Above: All versions of Windows allow for the use of log in passwords.

SECURING A LAPTOP

Because of the size of laptop hard drives and the different architecture used, something like remote wipe is not feasible for preventing access to a lost or stolen laptop. It would take too long to erase and would be ineffective if the laptop was not connected to the Internet, which could be too late to prevent the unauthorized copying of your data. However, there are other methods of preventing your files, folders and data from falling into the wrong hands.

Passwords

One of the first methods of ensuring your data is secure on a laptop is to set up a user account password. You do this in the same way as you set up a password on a desktop machine.

Above: Selecting User Accounts.

Windows Passwords

Different versions of Windows have slightly different methods of setting up passwords, but generally speaking, the following steps should give you a guide to the process.

1. Go into the Control Panel.

2. Select **User Accounts**, and select the account you want to password protect.

3. Select **Create a password**.

4. You will be asked to enter the new password twice, as well as a word or phrase to be used as a password hint.

5. Click **Create password**. The next time you boot up your computer, you will have to enter the password to gain access to your files and documents.

OS X Passwords

Different versions of OS X also vary in their password set-up procedures, but the following steps should give you an idea of how to do it. Note you have to be set up as an administrator to set passwords.

1. In the Apple menu, select **System Preferences**, and then click **Users & Groups**.

2. Click the lock icon and type in an administrator name and password, and then click **Unlock**.

3. Select the user you want, then the **Password** tab and then **Change Password**, or click **Login Options** to set various login options.

Above: New password screen.

Above: You can set a password as well as a security question or hint.

Hard Drive Encryption

To prevent the unauthorized copying and sending of your documents, files and folders, you can encrypt your laptop's hard drive. For modern versions of Windows, such as Windows 7 and Windows 8, you can use **Bitlocker** to encrypt your entire hard drive. For more information on using **Bitlocker**, *see* page 177. Later versions of Apple OS X also have an encryption facility called **FileVault**, which you can turn on in the **Security & Privacy** section in **System Preferences**.

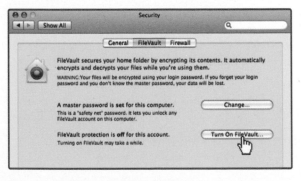

Above: Bitlocker in Windows 8.

Above: Turning on FileVault in OS X.

OTHER SECURITY MEASURES

You can download all sorts of apps and programs to help secure your smartphone, tablet or laptop.

○ **Mobile Defense (https://www. mobiledefense.com/):** An app available for Android phones that lets you remotely connect to your device, track its location and even remotely wipe data.

○ **Prey (https://preyproject.com/):** Designed for tracking and monitoring laptops and mobiles., you can even use it to activate the webcam on a laptop to take pictures of the thief.

○ **EXO5 (http://www.exo5.com/):** A business package designed to secure data on laptops by encrypting it as well as providing tracking information.

WIRELESS AND BLUETOOTH SECURITY

With mobile devices, you can connect to the internet anywhere and everywhere. However, this freedom comes with its own security risks, so it is important to know how to stay safe when using Wi-Fi, Bluetooth and public networks.

ACCESS ON THE GO

When the World Wide Web first emerged, the only way to access it was through a telephone wire. These days, there are various ways of getting online using a smartphone, laptop or tablet computer.

- **WAP:** Wireless Application Protocol is used by some mobile phones to download simplified web pages because they require less data than regular websites.

- **GPRS:** Either 2nd, 3rd or 4th generation (2G, 3G or 4G) General Packet Radio Service (GPRS) allows smartphones and tablets to connect to the Internet, download web pages or transfer data using mobile phone signals.

- **Wi-Fi:** You can also connect to the Internet using a wireless local area network. This can be your broadband connection at home or a public network.

Above: In locations that offer Wi-Fi access, you will usually see this symbol.

Hot Tip

Regardless of how you connect a mobile device to the Internet, always take basic security precautions, such as using HTTPS protocol when accessing email and banking services.

GPRS SECURITY

The radio signals that allow data transfer on mobile devices are pretty secure. Mobile telecoms companies use very sophisticated firewalls and encryption technology, which make unauthorized access extremely difficult.

WIRELESS ACCESS

The big downside to using GPRS data services is that mobile operators charge us for the data we download. However, if you are at home or in a location that has a public accessible network, you can access the Internet over Wi-Fi, which does not cost you anything for data transfer. However, unlike GPRS, Wi-Fi access does present some possible security issues.

What Is Wi-Fi?

Wi-Fi is simply the term used to describe wireless networking. Rather than plugging a laptop, smartphone or tablet into a broadband connection using a cable, Wi-Fi allows you to connect to the Internet using a localized radio signal.

Wireless Router

In order to connect wirelessly, you need access to a wireless router, which is plugged into a broadband connection and a wireless accessible device. Most smartphones, laptops and tablets now have in-built wireless adapters that allow you to connect to a wireless network.

Hot Tip

If your laptop does not have an in-built wireless adapter, you can use an external wireless adapter that plugs into the USB port, or a wireless card that can be installed inside the laptop.

WIRELESS SECURITY

As mentioned, while Wi-Fi offers us the freedom to connect to the Internet in all sorts of locations and download data at no cost, it does pose some security risks.

- **Device access**: Having Wi-Fi enabled on your device not only enables you to send data from your device, but also allows data to enter your device.

- **Hacking**: An unsecured wireless network could lead to somebody eavesdropping on the information you are sending and receiving.

- **Wi-Fi hotspots**: Anybody can set up a wireless hotspot, so you need to ensure you are on a trusted network.

Above: Wi-Fi hotpots are commonly found in cafés, pubs, airports and hotels.

Enabling Wi-Fi Access

In order to gain access to Wi-Fi, you normally have to enable Wi-Fi on the device. In order to keep your device secure, it is always a good idea to disable Wi-Fi when you are not using it. This will stop anybody connecting to your device without your knowledge (it will also prolong your battery life). Some devices such as mobile phones are often set up automatically to connect to wireless networks when they are in range, so it is worth browsing through your device's settings to disable this function.

Wi-Fi Hotspots

Wireless hotspots pose the biggest security risks when it comes to Wi-Fi, as it is difficult to know how secure the network is and whether the providers have any encryption in place to prevent hackers from eavesdropping on your data transfers. Most well-known wireless hotspot providers, such as coffee shop chains or hotels, provide information explaining their security protocols, so it is best to avoid hotspots from companies that cannot provide this information.

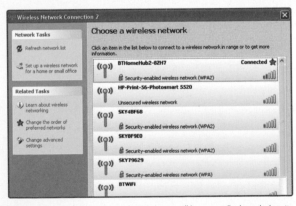

Above: You can disable Wi-Fi access in your network settings.

Above: A wireless connection with encryption will have a padlock symbol on it.

Wi-Fi Connection Security

Wi-Fi networks can be secured in a number of ways.

- **Wired Equivalency Privacy (WEP):** This is a form of encryption that ensures that any data you send or receive cannot be accessed by an unauthorized user. To access a WEP network, you will need to know the password, known as a WEP key.

- **Wi-Fi Protected Access (WPA and WPA2):** A newer and improved form of encryption compared to WEP, which is installed on some Windows machines.

- **Media Access Control (MAC):** Only allows devices approved by an administrator to connect to a wireless network.

Virtual Private Network (VPN)

No matter what the security employed by a public accessible network, you can never be too sure of who is listening in, as hackers can use a wide variety of tools and programs to

connect to the same network and eavesdrop on your data. For this reason, many businesses employ virtual private networks (VPNs) that encrypt all local web pages so that only authorized devices can access them.

Wi-Fi Privacy Tools

You can minimize the risk of using Wi-Fi hotspots by using a wide selection of privacy software.

○ **CyberGhost VPN (http://www.cyberg hostvpn.com/):** Allows you to set up your

Hot Tip

Be wary of 'evil twin' attacks, where hackers set up wireless hotspots (sometimes posing as reputable companies) so they access your passwords, login details and other information after you connect to their network.

own virtual private network every time you access the Internet and connects you to anonymous Internet servers.

- **HTPPS Everywhere (https://www.eff.org/https-everywhere/):** A plug-in for Firefox, Opera and Chrome Internet browsers that encrypts information from certain websites, such as Facebook, Twitter and Paypal.

- **Hotspot Shield (http://www.hotspotshield.com/):** Encrypts all your data every time you connect to the Internet.

Home Wi-Fi Security
Wi-Fi hotspots are not the only risk when using Wi-Fi on a mobile device. If you have Wi-Fi access at home, it is important to secure your network by employing the same encryption methods mentioned on page 196.

Above: Services like HTTPS Everywhere make using public Wi-Fi hotspots more secure.

BLUETOOTH SECURITY

Bluetooth is a similar technology to Wi-Fi. However, while Wi-Fi is mainly used as an access point to the Internet, Bluetooth is often used to connect devices together. Bluetooth enables speedy communication between different mobile devices, as well as allowing you to use wireless equipment such as headphones, microphones and hands-free systems. As with Wi-Fi, Bluetooth also comes with some security risks.

Above: Bluetooth-enabled devices will have this symbol on them.

How Bluetooth Works

Bluetooth uses radio signals to connect devices. This enables you to swap files with other Bluetooth users and connect devices to your smartphone. There are two steps to connecting a Bluetooth device.

- **Discoverability:** Devices have to find other Bluetooth devices within range. This is known as discoverability.

- **Pairing:** When two devices have discovered each other, they can be connected, known as pairing.

Connecting Devices

Normally, a user has to accept a pairing to his or her device. Some Bluetooth devices allow you to use PINs and passwords to prevent the unauthorized pairing of devices.

Securing Your Bluetooth Devices

Because Bluetooth tends to work at short ranges (about 10 metres), most people think they do not pose much of a security risk. However, hackers have found ways to access Bluetooth devices, allowing them to steal data, listen in on conversations and even make calls. There are steps you can take to prevent this.

Above: Turn Bluetooth off when you are not using it.

1. Set your Bluetooth devices to non-discoverable mode by default, which will prevent hackers from finding your device.

2. Never accept an unknown request to pair with your Bluetooth device.

3. Turn Bluetooth off when you are not using it.

4. Avoid using Bluetooth in crowded locations. Because Bluetooth requires users to be fairly close to one another, you are at greater risk of being hacked the more people there are around.

5. When exchanging data with somebody else, always request PIN and passwords to prevent a third party from hooking up.

MOBILE ANTIVIRUS, HACKING AND APP SECURITY

Desktop PCs are not the only devices that require antivirus software these days. Smartphones and tablets are equally at risk from malware and hackers, and many of these threats come from the apps we download and install.

THE RISE OF THE SMARTPHONE

Viruses on smartphones and tablets were unheard of a few years ago, but as the technology has become ubiquitous, malicious programmers and hackers have seen the potential that infecting these devices offers. After all, tablets and smartphones are just as capable as our desktops and laptops of accessing the Internet and running programs, so we store an awful lot of personal data on them, as well as using them to access sensitive websites such as online banks.

Mobile Architecture

Before we look at the malware threats and how you can prevent them, it is worth spending a moment to understand how smartphones and tablets work. Essentially, a tablet computer and smartphone use the same architecture. In other words, the operating system used on the latest iPhone is the same as the one used on the latest iPad.

Above: Tablet operating systems differ to those on laptops and PCs.

Mobile OS

There are numerous smartphone and tablet operating systems around, but the three most popular are:

- ○ **iOS**: Installed on Apple iPhones and iPads. Apple tend to bring out a newer version of their operating system whenever they release a new device.

- ○ **Android**: An operating system created by Google that runs on various manufacturers' tablets and smartphones.

- ○ **Windows Mobile/Phone**: Microsoft also produce operating systems for mobile devices; the first was Windows Mobile, then Windows Phone and now Windows 8.

Hot Tip

If you have a smartphone but want to buy a tablet, it will make your life easier to choose one that runs the same operating system, as it will allow greater interaction between the two devices.

APPS

The main difference between regular PCs and mobile devices such as smartphones and tablets is how they run programs. On mobile devices they are known as apps (short for applications), which are more self-contained than PC programs and are usually designed for just one specific task.

Installing Apps

Depending on your mobile operating system, apps are downloaded and installed from app stores.

- **Google Play (https:// play.google.com/):** Android apps are downloaded and installed from Google Play.

- **App Store (https://i tunes.apple.com/):** iOS users need to sign up to iTunes before they can download and install apps.

- **Windows (http://windows. microsoft.com/):** Has various app stores depending on the OS version.

- **Amazon (http://www. amazon. co.uk/appstore):** Owners of one of Amazon's Android-based tablets can download apps from the Amazon App Store.

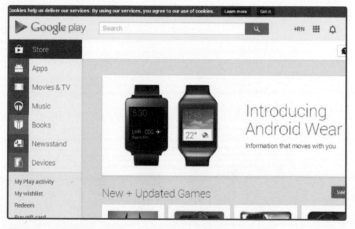

Above: You download apps from app stores such as Google Play.

Did You Know?

Most of the major app providers have their own app stores where you can download and install apps direct to your tablet or smartphone without using a web browser.

App Threats

You may think because big, reputable companies such as Apple and Google run their own app stores that everything on there will be safe and free from malware, but this is not the case. Anyone can make an app and upload it to these app stores, and while these companies strive to ensure everything listed is safe and free of malware, app threats still get through.

App Security

Apps range from functional apps, such as maps and shopping tools, to games and other fun items. Apps are usually cheap and many can be downloaded for free. Usually, these free apps are perfectly safe to use and malware free (they usually generate income from advertising), but some malicious developers have begun installing malware on apps, as well as creating pirated sub-standard or malware versions of legitimate apps. Because of this, you need to be a little cautious when downloading and installing apps to your smartphone or tablet.

Above: App reviews on Google Play.

- **Third-party app stores:** Stick to the major app stores and avoid downloading any app from a third-party website.

- **Reviews:** Read the reviews customers leave on app stores. If an app has lots of one-star reviews, it's a sign of something wrong.

- **Fakes:** Look out for fake versions of legitimate software, or brand new versions of existing apps. Visit the developers' web page to ensure you are getting a legitimate product.

App Permissions

When you install an app, you will often be asked to grant the app certain permissions, such as use of your Internet connection, access to your device's storage, and even access to GPS or other functions. Apps may even ask permissions for access to your SMS messages and email, which could be a sign of a malicious app, unless it is an email or SMS app that has a legitimate need for this access. Therefore, it may be worthwhile checking with the app store or with the developer directly to ensure they need the permissions that they do, and do not allow permissions on anything you think might be suspect.

MOBILE ANTIVIRUS

One way of identifying risky apps and keeping your phone or tablet free from malware is to install antivirus software. Not so long ago this was not seen as a necessity for smartphones and tablets, but as more and more malware is infecting mobile devices, so antivirus software is becoming as essential for mobile devices as it is on PCs.

Above: Antivirus software for mobiles and tablets often comes in the form of an app.

Antivirus Apps

Most of the major developers now produce antivirus solutions for mobile devices. Some offer free solutions, others sell yearly or monthly licences. However, mobile antivirus software is usually much cheaper than PC versions, and most software is sold in the form of an app.

- **Norton:** Produce antivirus apps for both Android and iOS, we well as multi-device support to protect all your devices. A free trial version is available on most app stores.

Hot Tip

Android devices are far more susceptible to malware than iOS and Windows devices, mainly because the operating system is open source, so it is available for anybody to develop apps for it.

Above: Avast have a free mobile suite for Android devices.

Above: Installing an antivirus app.

- **McAfee:** Also produce multi-platform antivirus for mobile devices as well as multi-device packages.

- **AVG:** Offer both a free and a professional version of antivirus software for Android devices. As well as malware protection, the app can help you locate a lost or stolen device and remote wipe its contents.

- **Avast:** Produce a free Android security suite, including malware protection, remote wipe and device location.

Installing Mobile Antivirus

Installing antivirus software on your tablet or smartphone is relatively straightforward.

1. Download the antivirus app, either direct from the developer or via an app store.

2. Install the app on your phone and approve the requested permissions.

3. Launch the antivirus app and follow the on-screen instructions.

4. For location and remote wipe services, you will need to register the device on the developer's website.

Removing Apps

Unlike PCs, app-based malware is unable to affect files and folders in the same way as a computer virus. However, malware can still copy and send data to third parties as well as spy on your online activities. However, if you suspect you have a malware threat, quite often the best way to resolve it is to uninstall any apps that you think could be the cause. You can always reinstall innocent apps once you have resolved any threat.

Parental Controls

As with desktop computers, you can limit what your children see on their smartphones or monitor their usage. Some mobile antivirus software comes complete with parental control software or you can download various apps.

- **PhoneSheriff (http://www.phonesheriff.com/):** Compatible with both Android and iOS, PhoneSheriff lets you restrict access to certain types of Internet content, as well as set time restrictions, block phone numbers and track the phone's location using GPS.

- **My Mobile Watchdog for Android (http://www.mymobilewatchdog.com/):** You can monitor, block, filter and track your child's Android or iOS device, but it does not offer a stealth mode, so your children will know they are being monitored.

- **Mobile Spy (http://www.mobile-spy.com/):** While you cannot block websites with Mobile Spy, you can see everything your children have been viewing, including deleted texts and emails.

- **Spyera (http://spyera.com/):** Has the advantage over other apps by letting you regulate and monitor your child's smartphone remotely. You can even listen in on calls.

MOBILE PHONE HACKING

While strictly not an Internet threat, mobile phone hacking has made the headlines in recent years due to some of the dubious methods employed by certain British newspapers. Mobile phone hacking is not actually very sophisticated but is the result of people not adequately securing their mobile phones.

Above: It takes just a few seconds to set up a voicemail PIN.

Voicemail PIN

The way people hack into voicemails is relatively simple. Most mobile phone companies provide a voicemail number that you can call from a landline phone to gain access to your messages. To prevent unauthorized access, a PIN is used, but most phones come with a factory default number, such as 1111, so unless you set a new PIN, a hacker can gain access to your messages.

Setting Voicemail PIN

The steps to set a new PIN will depend on your phone provider, but generally you need to do something approaching the following:

1. Using your mobile handset, call your voicemail service and listen for the option to change your PIN.

2. Press the appropriate button to change your PIN.

3. Enter your new PIN.

> ## Hot Tip
> If your voicemail suggests you have no new message when you know somebody has left one, or a new message suddenly disappears, it could be a sign that your mobile phone has been hacked.

SMARTPHONE AND TABLET SECURITY CHECKLIST

To summarize the points discussed in this chapter and to help you keep your mobile devices secure, here is a checklist.

- [ ] **Connections**: Disable Wi-Fi and Bluetooth when you are not using them.

- [ ] **Antivirus**: Install antivirus software on your smartphone and tablet.

- [ ] **Remote wipe**: Set up remote wipe in case your phone is lost or stolen.

- [ ] **PIN**: Make sure you change your voicemail PIN from the factory default.

- [ ] **Update**: Keep your operating system and apps updated.

- [ ] **Apps**: Be careful when downloading and installing apps.

- [ ] **Hotspots**: Be wary of using public access points.

- [ ] **HTTPS**: Always use HTTPS for email and other secure online activities, or think about setting up a VPN (virtual private network).

- [ ] **Device**: Keep tabs on your device. Never leave it unattended, even for a moment.

ADVANCED TROUBLESHOOTING

RECOVERING LOST DATA

If you are unfortunate enough to have your computer infected by a virus or hacked, cleaning and protecting your system may be only part of the solution. Many people find that malware and hackers erase important data and files, and getting those back can be a struggle.

DATA LOSS

Following a malware or hacking attack, one of the worst outcomes can be the loss of data; photographs, documents or all those important emails could have vanished. However, all is not lost. Computer files are rarely completely erased, although it may seem that way, and it is sometimes possible to get your data back.

Hot Tip

Before you try to recover any lost data, it is essential that you are confident any malware has been removed from your system, otherwise a virus could end up deleting the data again, this time permanently.

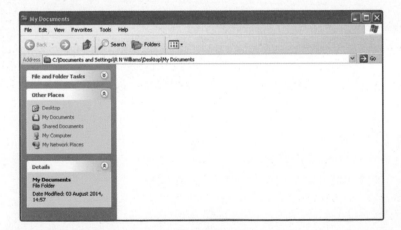

Cause of Wiped Data

Before you can go about trying to recover files, it is important to understand how they came to be erased in the first place. Erased data can be caused by a number of events.

Left: You may find all your documents have gone following a virus attack.

- **Antivirus**: Your antivirus software may have deleted or quarantined a file to remove a malware infection.

- **Viruses**: Some viruses delete files as part of their programming.

- **Deliberate erasing**: A hacker with access to your machine could deliberately wipe your data for malicious reasons.

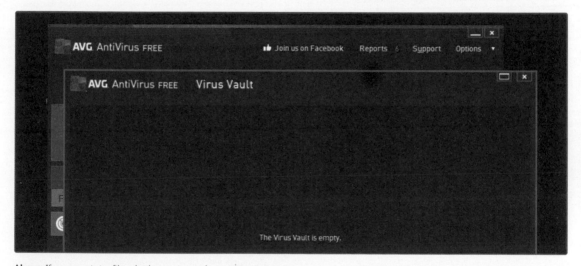

Above: If you are missing files, check your virus vault or antivirus quarantine.

Quarantined Items

The first place to check if you have lost a file is your antivirus quarantine. Normally, antivirus software tries to clean an infected file, but if it cannot, it places it in quarantine where it cannot do any more harm. However, before you can retrieve your file, you need to ensure it does not pose a threat as you could just be unleashing the virus back onto your system.

Recovering Quarantined Files

Most antivirus software makes it simple to release files from quarantine. In most cases, you simply right click and select **Restore** and the file is returned to its original location on the drive. However, if the file is still infected, you will receive a warning message and the antivirus software may put it back in quarantine. Most antivirus software will let you exclude files from antivirus protection, but you should only do this if you think the antivirus is giving a false positive and the file is actually safe.

Above: Cloud storage services such as Dropbox let you back up all your important files to the Internet.

RECOVERING FROM A BACKUP

By far the simplest ways to recover data following a virus or hacker attack is to retrieve the file from a backup, whether a removable media device, such as a flash drive, or from cloud storage, but first, you need to ensure the backup version is not also infected.

Scanning Removable Media

Most antivirus software will automatically scan a removable media device as soon as it is inserted into the computer or tablet. If yours is not set up to do this, follow these steps.

1. To restore backups from a flash drive or other removable media, insert in into your computer.

2. Once your operating system has recognized the device, on a Windows machine, go into the **My Computer** folder and right click and choose antivirus scan from the menu; on an Apple device, hold down the mouse button and select scan.

3. Your antivirus software will let you know if there is an infection and clean the files.

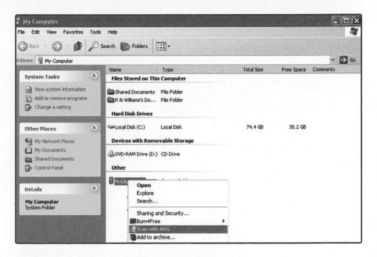

Above: Scanning a movable hardware device with AVG.

RECOVERING CHANGED EXTENSION FILES

Due to the way computers erase files (more on this in a bit), malware rarely deletes files completely, but in order to prevent you from using files, they sometimes change the file extensions (the application suffix, such as '.doc', '.jpg'). Often this is done by changing the file into a shortcut, which will not open, making you think the file is lost for ever. This is very common with infected files stored on removable media, but you can normally convert the file extension back.

Recovering Changed Extension Files

1. First, if the software is on removable media, scan it using your antivirus software to clean any viruses from it.

Above: Running the command prompt.

2. Run the command prompt. In Windows 7/8, type **cmd** in the Start screen. In Windows XP, click **Start**, select **Run** and then type **cmd**.

3. In the black console screen, type: **ATTRIB -H -R -S /S /D [drive letter:] *.*** replacing [drive letter:] with the letter of the drive where your infected file is, such as E:.

```
C:\WINDOWS\system32\cmd.exe

:rosoft Windows XP [Version 5.1.2600]
> Copyright 1985-2001 Microsoft Corp.

\Documents and Settings\R M Williams>ATTRIB -H -R -S /S /D E:\*.*_
```

Above: Restoring file extensions in drive E: using the command prompt.

4. Press **Enter**. Now, when you open your file folder, your files should be present and correct.

Hot Tip

If you cannot clean an infected flash drive or change file extensions using the command prompt, check the file extensions are not Read Only (right click and Properties).

TEMPORARY FILES

Not everybody backs up their computer regularly, which means if data is lost due to a virus or hacking attack, getting it back can be problematic. However, it is not impossible and the first thing to do is check for any temporary files.

Autosave and Temporary Files

Some programs, such as Microsoft Office, have an autosave and recovery system that automatically saves versions of your documents. Even if you do not have the autosave function on, programs such as Microsoft Office create temporary files while you are working, and these can be used to recover lost documents.

Finding Temporary Files

Temporary and autosave files can be recognized by a tilde (˜) followed by a few letters, such as ˜wrdxxxx.tmp. You can usually alter the settings in your programs to save temporary files to any location you like, but most people never change these settings. These locations vary depending on the program, but in Microsoft Word, for instance, temporary and autosave files can be found.

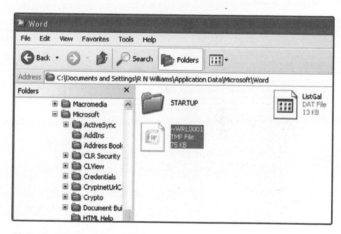

Above: A temporary document file for Microsoft Word.

- **Windows 7 and 8**: You can find temporary Word files in either **C:\Users\<username>\AppData\Local\Microsoft\Word** or **C:\Users\<username>\AppData\Local\Temp**

- **Windows XP/98/95**: In older versions of Windows look in either **C:\Documents and Settings\<username>\Application Data** and the program folder applicable to the file or **C:\Documents and Settings\<username>\Local Settings\Temp**

Hidden Files

Temporary files are stored as hidden files, so in order to see them you need to have the temporary folders set for viewing hidden files.

1. Open Windows Explorer (**Start**, **Programs**, **Accessories**, **Windows Explorer**) and browse for the folder where you think your temporary files may be stored.

2. Select **Tools** from the folder menu bar and scroll down to **Folder Options**.

3. Select the **View** tab. Scroll down to the **Hidden files and folders** option, and check the button next to **Show hidden files or folders**. Click Apply.

Above: Showing hidden files and folders.

Opening Temporary and Autosave Files

When you have found a temporary or autosave file, you need to open it to see if there is any data on it. However, you cannot simply double click it as you would to open a normal file; you have to tell Windows what program you want to use to open the file.

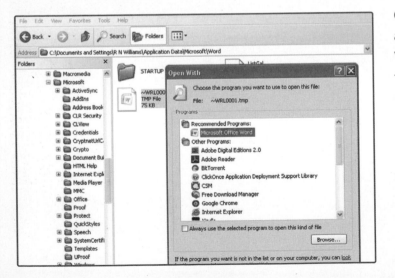

Left: Choosing a program to open a temporary file.

1. Right click the file and choose
    Open With.

2. Select the program you want to use
    from the list, or select **Choose Program**
    if it is not listed.

3. Alternatively, you can drag and drop the
    folder into an open program window.

RECOVERY SOFTWARE TOOLS

If you have no backup, and there is no temporary file to help you out, you may think all is lost,
but that may not necessarily be so, as you can use a wide variety of software tools to search
for lost files on your computer.

How Computers Erase Files

When you delete a file (and empty the recycle
bin), you may think the file has been deleted
for ever; however, computers never actually
delete files. What normally happens is that the
location on the hard drive where the file is
stored is marked as accessible, allowing other
data to overwrite it, but that can take weeks,
months or even years, so your file can linger
on the hard drive for a long time.

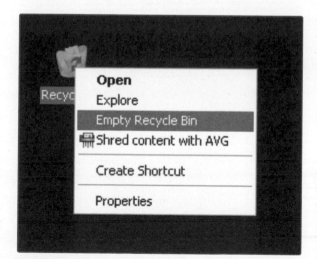

Recovering Erased Files

A number of different software solutions are
available for all sorts of platforms: PCs, Macs,

Above: When you empty a recycle bin, you may think the data
is gone for ever, but that may not be the case.

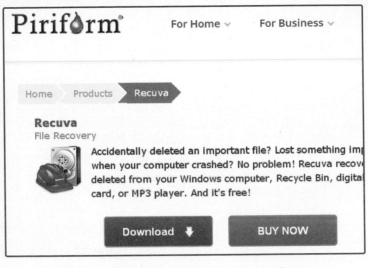

Above: Recuva is a simple-to-use program for recovering lost data.

tablets and smartphones. These can help you restore files that you thought were deleted or erased forever.

- **Recuva (http://www.piriform.com/recuva):** A free and very easy-to-use Windows program that lets you restore all sorts of deleted files from documents and photographs to emails and music files.

- **Disk Drill (http://www.cleverfiles.com/):** A Mac OS X tool that not only lets you recover deleted files but also protects important files from accidental deletions. There is both a basic free version and a paid-for version with added functionality.

- **EaseUS (http://www.easeus.com/):** Sells recovery software for Windows, OS X, Android and IOS.

- **VirtualLab (http://www.binarybiz.com/):** A recovery system for Windows or OS X machines that lets you restore files from hard drives as well as from CD and DVDs.

- **File Scavenger (http://www.quetek.com/prod02.htm):** A simple but highly effective Windows tool for finding and recovering lost files.

- **Active File Recovery (http://www.file-recovery.com/):** Sells a number of file recovery solutions for Windows, OS X and mobile devices.

SECURING ERASED DATA

While software that can recover deleted files may be useful when you have been the victim of data loss, they do pose another security threat. If you change your computer, or install a new hard drive, the last thing you want is your personal information, files and data on your old computer or hard drive falling into the wrong hands. Because of this, many of the hitherto mentioned file recovery platforms also offer secure delete functions that let you erase data completely from your hard drive or removable media.

DATA RECOVERY SERVICES

If you have tried every possible method of recovering deleted files and failed, do not dismay. You may be able to find a data recovery specialist in your area who may be able to help. These people use specialist equipment and software to retrieve your data, even when all other methods have failed. Many also offer secure and permanent erasing of old hard drives.

Left: Antivirus software can help you permanently erase data.

Hot Tip

Some antivirus software have facilities that let you permanently erase files or folders, but you need to exercise caution when using them, as once the file is deleted, it is gone for ever.

SYSTEM REPAIR

Viruses and malware can not only erase files, but they can also make your machine unstable, causing system crashes, even preventing you from booting up your computer.

SYSTEM STABILITY

If you have had malware on your computer, even if you have managed to clean the infection using antivirus software, you may find things have become a little unstable. System crashes, booting problems and other issues can often occur following a malware attack. Viruses and other malware may have corrupted system files, and while your antivirus software may have removed the threat, most cannot repair registry files and other operating system information used by your computer.

```
A problem has been detected and Windows has been shut down to prev
to your computer.

The problem seems to be caused by the following file: kbdhid.sys

MANUALLY_INITIATED_CRASH

If this is the first time you've seen this stop error screen,
restart your computer. If this screen appears again, follow
these steps:

Check to make sure any new hardware or software is properly instal
If this is a new installation, ask your hardware or software manuf
for any Windows updates you might need.

If problems continue, disable or remove any newly installed hardwa
or software. Disable BIOS memory options such as caching or shadow
If you need to use safe mode to remove or disable components, rest
your computer, press F8 to select Advanced Startup Options, and th
select Safe Mode.

Technical Information:

*** STOP: 0x000000e2 (0x00000000, 0x00000000, 0x00000000, 0x000000

*** kbdhid.sys - Address 0x94efd1aa base at 0x94efb000 DateStamp 0
```

Above: The so-called 'blue screen of death' is a common symptom following a virus infection.

System Tools

Fortunately, when it comes to desktop PCs, Macs and laptops running OS X or Windows, you have a wide variety of tools at your disposal that can help restore things to the way they were before the malware struck. These range from tools that scan your hard drives and system for potential errors, to those that roll things back to a time before the infection, restoring your system.

WINDOWS TOOLS

Windows has a number of tools that can help you repair your system registry.

○ **Scandisk:** Will scan hard drives for potential errors and corrupted files.

○ **Safe Mode:** Designed for troubleshooting, Safe Mode boots up a limited version of Windows with only the minimum of files installed.

○ **System Restore:** Lets you roll back the operating system to a previous state.

Scandisk

Performing a scan of your hard drive is relatively easy.

1. Click **Start** and select **My Computer**.

2. Right click on the drive you want to scan and select **Properties**.

3. Click the **Tools** tab and under **Error Checking**, click the **Check now** button.

4. In the window, select whether you want to fix errors automatically or not (Windows 7 and later), then hit **Start**.

Safe Mode

If your machine simply will not boot up, you can try starting in Safe Mode and then run Scandisk once Windows has booted up.

Hot Tip

If your computer crashes, Windows will automatically run Scandisk and check the hard drive for errors when it boots up.

Above: Click the Check Now option under Tools in Properties to scan your computer with Scandisk.

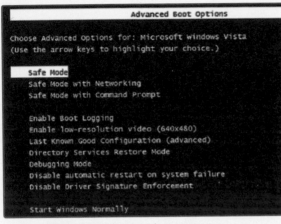

Above: Safe Mode menu in boot options.

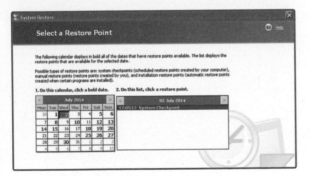

Above: Choosing a system restore point.

> # Hot Tip
> Unfortunately, Android and iOS devices do not have a system repair and restore option, but you can do a factory reset to restore the device to its default settings, but you will lose all your data and files.

1. Press and hold the F8 key as your computer starts.

2. Select **Safe Mode** in the options window.

System Restore

System Restore can return your PC's system files and programs to a time when everything was working well. Programs installed after a restore point will be removed, but System Restore will not remove files, so you will not lose data.

1. Click **Start**, **Programs**, **Accessories**, **System Tools**, and then select **System Restore**.

2. On the Welcome to System Restore page, check the **Restore my computer to an earlier time** button.

3. Click **Next**, then choose a **System Checkpoint** on the calendar. Remember to choose a date before your computer started having issues.

4. Click **Next**, read the warnings about saving data and closing programs, and then click **Next** to restore Windows to your chosen time.

OS X TROUBLESHOOTING

Mac computers have similar methods of repairing and restoring the operating system to Windows machines.

Disk Utility

Disk Utility repairs and restores OS X systems, but you do need the installation disk to make use of it.

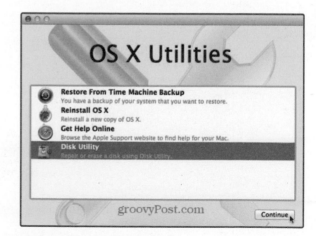

1. Turn off the computer and insert the OS X installation disk.

2. Hold down the **C** key to load the set-up program. Choose your language to continue.

3. In the menu, select **Disk Utility**.

Above: OS X Utilities include Disk Utility.

4. Select the **First Aid** tab and check the disclosure triangle to display the names of your hard disk volumes.

5. Select which volume you wish to check and click **Repair**. Disk Utility will check and repair the disk before rebooting your Mac.

Mac Safe Boot

You can also boot up a Mac in safe mode to troubleshoot any issues.

1. Turn on your Mac, and after you hear the start-up tone, press and hold the Shift key.

2. Release the Shift key when you see the Apple logo and the progress indicator (looks like a spinning gear).

3. The Mac will now boot up in safe mode.

Below: Mac Safe Boot.

OS X Recovery

In later versions of OS X, you can hold down **Command R** during start-up to run OS X Recovery. This is full of restore and repair utilities, such as Disk Utility. It also lets you erase your hard drive, reinstall a new version of OS X, or restore your Mac from a backup.

Time Machine

Time Machine is the built-in backup feature of OS X that lets you restore your Mac to a previous time. You do need an external drive to use Time Machine, but it is worth the investment, because you can automatically back up your entire system, including system files, applications, preferences, email messages and all your documents and multimedia.

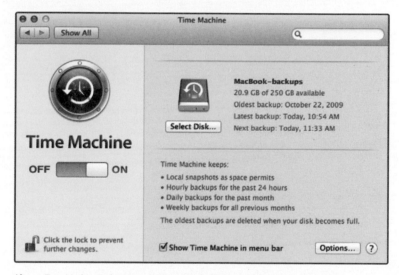

Above: Time Machine makes it easy to back up your entire system.

WINDOWS REGISTRY REPAIR

Common issues that affect Windows machines following a malware attack have to do with the system registry. The registry contains all the settings and configurations for the operating system, so when there is a problem in the registry, Windows can suffer from instability and crashes, but you may be able to rectify the situation by using one of a variety of registry tools.

Windows Registry Checker

Whenever a Windows machine has successfully booted up, the Windows Registry Checker makes a backup copy of the system files and registry settings, which can be used to repair registry entries. While Windows Registry Checker automatically scans the registry when a machine is booting up, if you have a registry issue and need to start in Safe Mode, you may need to manually run Registry Checker.

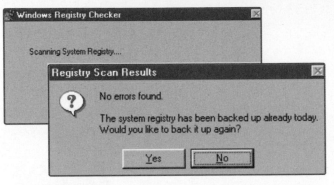

Above: The Windows Registry Checker will automatically fix issues with the registry.

1. Click **Start**, and then **Run**.

2. In the box, type **scanregw.exe**, and then click OK to run Registry Checker, which will scan and automatically repair your registry.

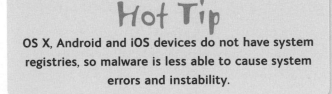

Hot Tip

OS X, Android and iOS devices do not have system registries, so malware is less able to cause system errors and instability.

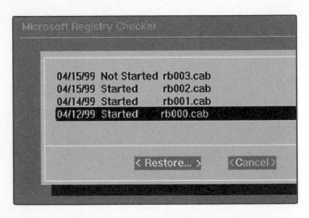

Above: You can choose from multiple registry restore points.

Restoring Registry

If after running Windows Registry Checker, you still have issues, it may because the backup file Windows is using is also corrupted. To fix this, you can restore from an earlier registry backup.

1. Run the command prompt. In Windows 7/8, type **cmd** in the Start screen; in Windows XP, click **Start**, select **Run**, and then type **cmd**.

2.   Type **scanregw.exe/restore**.

3.   Restore from one of the five registry backup files listed.

Registry Tools

As well as Windows Registry Checker, you can download and install a variety of registry cleaning and repair tools that may help get your registry back to a stable condition.

○   **CCleaner (https://www.piriform.com/CCLEANER):** A free registry-cleaning program that will fix invalid or corrupted entries.

○   **Wise Registry Cleaner (http://www.wisecleaner.com/):** Another free registry-repair tool that can be used on Windows 8, 7, Vista and XP.

Operating System Repair

You can also repair your operating system by using your installation disc. In Mac OS X machines, this is done using Disk Utility (*see* pages 225–26) and selecting **Repair Disk** from the menu. In Windows, repairing the OS is done in a similar manner.

1.   Put your Windows disk into your drive and restart the computer.

2.   On the **Install Windows** screen, select language, time and keyboard, and then click **Next**.

3.   Select **Repair Your Computer**.

4.   In **System Recovery Options**, select **Startup Repair** and click **Next**.

Above: The installation screen does differ on different versions of Windows, but there is always a repair option.

REINSTALLING THE OPERATING SYSTEM

If you have run into problems trying to repair your registry, or your operating system is still unstable, the only recourse may be to reinstall your operating system. However, whether you have a Mac or PC, reinstalling an operating system can bring with it a few problems. In some instances, you may lose data, user accounts and saved preferences, so before you consider a reinstallation make sure you back up all important files and folders.

Hot Tip

If your Windows PC will not install from disc, you may have to change the boot order in the BIOS settings (placing CD/DVD before hard drive). To access, restart your computer and follow the prompt that says: Press <key> to enter setup.

Windows Reinstallation

Reinstallation of a Windows machine is pretty straightforward.

Above: Reinstalling Windows Vista.

1. Insert the installation disk into your computer drive.

2. Turn off your computer.

3. Reboot and press a key when prompted.

4. Your computer should run the installation disk, so follow all on-screen instructions to reinstall your version of Windows.

Reinstalling OS X

When your Mac is booting up, you can reinstall OS X from within the operating system.

1. Insert the installation disk into your computer, and wait for it to appear on your desktop.

2. Double click the **Install Mac OS X** icon, and then click **Restart**.

3. OS X will now reinstall.

Non-booting Install

If your Mac will not boot up at all, you can reinstall OS X when you reboot as follows.

1. Turn on the computer, holding down the **Option** key.

2. **Start-up Manager** will begin where you will see all of the sources from which you can reboot.

3. Insert the OS X installation disk. After a few moments, the DVD will appear on the list of sources. Select the installation disk to reboot and reinstall OS X.

4. Follow all on-screen instructions during the reinstallation process.

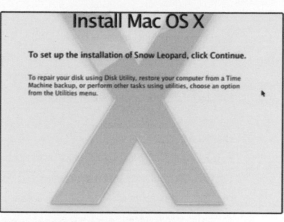

Above: Reinstalling Max OS X Snow Leopard.

Above: Installing OS X from a disk.

Hot Tip

If you are restoring an OS X operating system, avoid using Migration Assistant. This is good for upgrading OS X but it will only restore your machine to the way it was, which defeats the purpose of a reinstallation.

THE LAST RESORT

If all the repair and reinstallation options have failed, you may be able to reformat your hard drive and reinstall your OS from scratch. Reformatting will erase everything on your hard drive, which will mean you will have to reinstall not just the operating system, but also all your files, folders, programs and system drivers.

Backing Up

Before you consider reformatting, you need to back up all your files. This means not just your documents, pictures and multimedia, but you also need to ensure you have copies of your system drivers (software that enables your hardware to run), programs and anything else you may lose when your hard drive is wiped.

Windows Reformatting

On Windows machines, there are two choices when it comes to reformatting.

Above: You can run a format on a second hard drive in Windows by right clicking and selecting format.

○ **Quick format:** Does not check the drive for its condition. In addition, the data is not erased, but simply marked as being writable (new data can take its place).

○ **Full format:** Will check the hard drive for any bad sectors; it then erases all data on the drive.

Partitions

When a hard disk is formatted, it has to be assigned a drive letter, such as C:. This is done by means of a partition. Most computers have single partitions, so the letter C represents the entire hard disk, but you can have multiple partitions.

Reformatting a Windows PC

Once you have backed up your computer, you can reformat and reinstall your Windows operating system. To reformat a Windows hard drive, insert your Windows installation disk into the drive and reboot your computer.

1. At the **Welcome to Setup** page, press **Enter**, and then **F8** to accept the licensing agreement and press **Esc** to bypass Windows repair.

2. Use the arrow keys either to create a new partition or to use your current one. For a full format, it is best to create a new partition.

3. Select the partition where you want to install Windows, then press **Enter**.

Above: Creating a partition before formatting.

4. Select the format options (quick or full), then the files system option; for most recent versions of Windows, it is recommended to use a NTFS file system.

5. Press **Enter** to reformat the drive. Once complete, you will have to reinstall your operating system by rebooting and following the instruction on the installation disk.

Above: Choosing partition options.

| First Aid | Erase | Partition | RAID | Restore |

Volume Scheme:

Current ⇕

Macintosh HD

Volume Information

Name: Macintosh HD

Format: Mac OS Extended (Journaled) ⇕

Size: 116.12 GB

To erase and partition the selected disk, choose a volume scheme, set options for each volume, and click Apply. To resize the volumes on the selected disk, drag the dividers between them and click Apply.

This volume will not be erased.
Size: 85.5 GB
Available space: 11.2 GB

Above: Entering name and size for partition.

| First Aid | Erase | Partition | RAID | Restore |

To erase a disk, select a disk or volume, select the appropriate format and name and click the erase button.

• Erasing a disk results in all volumes of that disk being erased and one large volume being created on that disk.
• Erasing a volume results in a clean volume being created.
• Erasing an optical disc (CD-RW, DVD-RW, etc.) will result in a blank optical disc. No format is applied to an erased optical disc.

Volume Format: Mac OS Extended (Journaled) ⇕

Name: Untitled

☐ Install Mac OS 9 Disk Driver

If this option is not selected, this device cannot be used by a computer running Mac OS 9. This option does not affect Classic.

Above: Selecting erase.

Hot Tip

For owners of OS X 10.7 Lion and later, you do not need an installation disk to run Disk Utility; hold the Command and R keys after you hear the start-up tone.

Reformatting a Mac

To reformat a hard drive on a Mac, you need to use Disk Utility (*see* pages 225–26).

1. Select your Mac's hard drive and select **Partition**.

2. In the Partition Information box, enter a name for your hard drive and the size of partition.

3. Click **Apply**, and then click **Partition**.

4. Go back to the **Disk Utility** main menu and select the partition you have just created.

5. Select **Erase** (ensure that the format is Mac OS Extended, which is set by default).

6. Select a security option. The securer the option, the more thorough it will be in erasing your data, but it will also be slower.

7. Once formatting is complete, reinstall your OS X operating system.

REMOVING STUBBORN THREATS

Some malware can be really stubborn when it comes to cleaning a computer. Either they act like normal programs so antivirus software does not spot them, or they infect areas that make them hard to remove. In these instances, you may have to take care of the threat manually.

IDENTIFYING THREATS

If your antivirus scan comes up clean, you may still feel that your machine is infected with something because of the way it is acting: your PC may be running slowly, your Internet browser playing up, or some other symptom is indicating something is not quite right. If this is the case, you may have to do a bit of diagnosis to identify what the problem is.

BROWSER THREATS

One of the most common threats missed by antivirus software is malware installed into browser extensions. Extensions, plug-ins, browser helper objects (BHOs) and add-ons are tools designed to expand the functionality of your web browser, but some malicious software developers use these to install adware and other malware.

Extensions

Extensions (8)

Chrome MineSweeper - Version: 0.3
A Classic MineSweeper game with beautiful graphics and score board
Disable - Uninsta

Chromed Bird - Version: 1.5.0
Chromed Bird is a Twitter extension that allows you to follow your timelines and interact with your Twitter account.
Disable - Uninsta

Digg for Chrome - Version: 0.9
See what is being discovered and shared on Digg
Disable - Uninsta

Google Translate - Version: 1.1.5
This extension translates entire webpages into a language of your choice with one click. By the Google Translate team.
Disable - Uninsta

Google Wave Notifier - Version: 2.2
Displays number of unread Waves.
Disable - Uninsta

IE Tab - Version: 1.0.11208.1
Display web pages using IE in a tab
Disable - Uninsta

Above: Extensions can be really useful, but they can also harbour malware.

Browser Helper Objects

Browser helper objects (BHOs) are plug-ins for Internet Explorer designed to allow the browser to display file formats it could not otherwise interpret. However, they can also harbour malware, so if your browser seems to have a mind of its own, you may want to disable your BHOs to see if they are the cause.

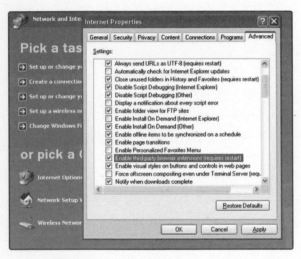

Above: Disabling browser extensions.

1. Close Internet Explorer, click **Start**, **Settings** and **Control Panel**.

2. Select **Internet Options** and click the **Advanced** tab.

3. Under **Browsing**, clear the **Enable third-party browser extensions** check box.

4. Restart Internet Explorer.

Removing BHOs

If Internet Explorer starts to function normally after disabling your browser extensions, you know a BHO is the cause of the problem. Therefore you may want to run a BHO removal tool to identify and remove the offending BHO. Many of these can be found on the Internet.

Extensions and Plug-ins

Internet Explorer is not the only browser plagued by malware threats hidden in plug-ins.

> ## Hot Tip
>
> **Spy BHO Remover (http://securityxploded.com/ bhoremover.php) is an easy-to-use removal tool that will identify known BHO threats and remove them.**

Most browsers rely on extensions to improve your web experience, and they can all too easily be hijacked by malicious malware. However, disabling and removing extensions and plug-ins can be pretty simple.

Above: Spy BHO Remover can remove malware posing as browser helper objects.

1. Go into your browser settings.

2. In Firefox click the **Add-ons** button, in Chrome, click the **Extensions** link on the left, in Opera select **Extensions** from the tools menu.

3. In Firefox, select **Extensions or Appearance** in the **Add-ons Manager** tab, and click the **Disable** button next to the extension you want to disable.

4. In Chrome, simply uncheck the **Enable** box to disable the extension.

Above: You can enable and disable most extension quite easily.

5. In Opera, disable extensions in the **Manage Extensions** menu.

Stubborn Extensions

Some extensions, such as Enterprise Policy extensions, which were created by Google to help developers, differ from normal extensions in that they cannot be removed or disabled in the normal way on Windows machines (OS X users can still delete them). This has made them a popular tool for malware producers, who can use them to install adware.

Above: Extensions with long random IDs that cannot be removed are usually malware.

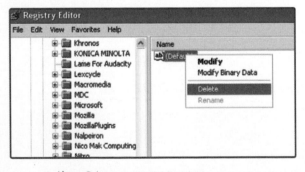

Above: Searching for an extensions registry entry.

Above: Deleting an extension in registry.

Removing Stubborn Browser Malware

If you have an extension that you cannot remove in the Extensions page, it is possible to get rid of them, although it is a fairly complicated procedure.

1. Go into the Control Panel and select the **Install/Uninstall Programs**.

2. Select anything that you do not remember installing and uninstall it. In particular, look for any programs with the words 'ad', 'blocker' or 'coupon' in the title.

3. Go into your extension manager in your browser, and make a note of the name of the extension that you want to remove.

4. Do a search (**Start**, **Search**) and type or paste in the name of the extension. Delete any folders or files that come up in the search.

5. Run the Registry Editor (regedit.exe), click **Edit** and select **Find next**.

6. Type or paste in the ID of the extension and press the **Find next** button.

7. After the search, you should see the extension listed in the folder called: HKEY_LOCAL_MACHINE \SOFTWARE\ Policies\ Google\Chrome\ Extension InstallForcelist

8. Right click on the number to the left of the extension name, and from the menu, select **Delete** and confirm you want to delete it.

9. Finally, open Google Chrome, and type in **chrome://policy/** in the address bar, and then in the window click on **Show Value**. You should see the location of the extension data folder, such as C:/ProgramData/Adblocker. Go to this location and delete the folder.

SYSTEM THREATS

Your browser is not the only location where you can find threats that your antivirus may have missed. If you really want to be sure your PC is virus free, it Is worth checking the system files, particularly those installed on start-up, as this is a common place for viruses and Trojans to linger.

1. Click **Start**, **Run**, and then type in **msconfig** to run the System Configuration Utility.

> # Hot Tip
> Software such as Malwarebytes can remove stubborn browser extensions: http://www. malwarebytes.org/

Above: Google policy values show you the address of the offending extension on your hard drive.

Above: Start-up files in the System Configuration Utility.

2. Click on the **Startup** tab. Here is a list of all the items that run when the machine boots up. Note anything suspicious, such as those with **Unknown** listed under the manufacturer or those claiming to be Windows or Microsoft files.

Removing Start-up Viruses

1. Disable the suspicious file in the System Configuration Utility (check the box and click **Disable**).

Above: The potential location of a virus.

2. Reboot your computer in Safe Mode and run **msconfig** again. If the threat is still there, you can be pretty sure it is a virus.

3. Note down the location of the virus, and then run Registry Editor.

4. Go to the location of the virus and right click the suspected file, select **modify** and put ':' in front of the value data. This will disable the virus but not delete it.

5. Reboot your computer in normal mode. If all is well you can be assured the file is not important to your system, so go back into Registry Editor and delete the virus (right click **Delete**).

6. Reboot again, and then run **msconfig** to check that the threat has been removed.

Above: Modifying registry values.

ROGUE PROGRAMS AND SECURITY TOOLS

Some of the simplest malware can also be the hardest for antivirus software to spot and remove. Sometimes they are in the form of innocent programs that install themselves on start-up, or they might be in the guise of a security tool, which provides false scans prompting you to pay to have fake threats removed.

Hot Tip

After making changes to your registry, it is a good idea to run a registry-cleaning program such as CClean or Wise Registry Cleaner to fix any issues or corrupted files (*see* page 229).

Processes

In order to see if you have a rogue program or security tool running on your Windows machine, you need to open the Task Manager (**Ctrl**, **Alt**, **Delete**), in OS X use the Activity Monitor (**Applications**, **Utilities**).

1. Make a note of any suspicious processes. Look for processes with no clearly defined name, such as a random number or string of letters.

2. Do an Internet search of these processes to see if they are malware; if there is no record of any process with the same name, it is unlikely to be genuine.

3. If so, **Force Quit** the process in **Task Manager/Activity Monitor**.

4. Do a search for files and data associated with the name of that program. Remove any associated files or folders.

Image Name	User Name	CPU	Mem Usage
vlc.exe	R N Williams	02	11,332 K
smax4pnp.exe	R N Williams	00	584 K
avgui.exe	R N Williams	00	12,652 K
wltray.exe	R N Williams	00	924 K
NOTEPAD.EXE	R N Williams	00	708 K
avgidsagent.exe	SYSTEM	00	11,948 K
spoolsv.exe	SYSTEM	00	1,236 K
bcmwltry.exe	SYSTEM	00	1,008 K
wltrysvc.exe	SYSTEM	00	68 K
NVSVC32.EXE	SYSTEM	00	596 K
NLSSRV32.EXE	SYSTEM	00	64 K
svchost.exe	LOCAL SERVICE	00	916 K
svchost.exe	NETWORK SERVICE	00	1,620 K
NitroPDFDriverSe...	SYSTEM	00	52 K
avgemcx.exe	SYSTEM	00	168 K
svchost.exe	SYSTEM	00	13,304 K
svchost.exe	NETWORK SERVICE	00	1,184 K
svchost.exe	SYSTEM	00	1,012 K
lsass.exe	SYSTEM	00	1,724 K
services.exe	SYSTEM	00	1,612 K
winlogon.exe	SYSTEM	00	704 K
CSRSS.EXE	SYSTEM	00	3,932 K
AVGCSRVX.EXE	SYSTEM	00	79,748 K
AVGRSX.EXE	SYSTEM	00	2,516 K

Above: Using Task Manager to identify possible threats.

HARDWARE SECURITY

Not all Internet security comes in software form. You can get all sorts of hardware to help secure your computers and Internet connection, which can be especially useful if you have a home or small-business network.

ROUTERS

The router is the hardware device through which you connect to the Internet. Because of this, the router can be your first line of defence against online threats, hackers and other Internet nasties. Routers have all sorts of in-built security measures, but in order to take advantage of them, you need to set up your router correctly.

Types of Router

Routers come in a variety of types, but for most people there are two basic choices.

Above: Most people use wireless routers these days.

○ **Wired routers:** Less common for home networking these days, but wired routers are more secure and so preferred by most business networks, although they are less flexible.

○ **Wireless routers:** Let you connect devices wirelessly to the router, giving greater freedom; the most common choice for most home networks.

Understanding Routers

In order to make the best of your router and its security features, it is worth understanding how a router works and what its core functions are.

○ **Packet forwarding**: Internet traffic travels around in small packets of data. It is the router's job to relay these packets to you.

○ **Packet filtering**: Not all data travelling to your network is wanted. Routers sift through the packets and filter what is and isn't required.

○ **Packet switching**: Routers break data into packets and send them separately, to be reassembled at the destination.

HARDWARE FIREWALLS

Because a router's main job is to sift through the data coming into your home, it is very easy for it to act like a firewall. In fact, most wireless routers now have a firewall option, but if your router does not, you can also buy a specialized hardware firewall.

Hot Tip

Having a hardware firewall does not mean you do need a software one too. If you take a device out of your home, your hardware firewall can no longer protect it.

ACCESSING YOUR ROUTER

To understand whether your router has a firewall installed, or if you wish to turn it on, you must first access your router or hardware firewall's configuration settings. Most come with software that you can install on your hard drive to access the functions, but this is actually not required, and the simplest way to reach your router or firewall's configuration settings is to open an Internet browser and enter the device's IP address in the address bar. You can normally find this on a sticker attached to your device. If you cannot find it, go online and visit your manufacturer's support pages.

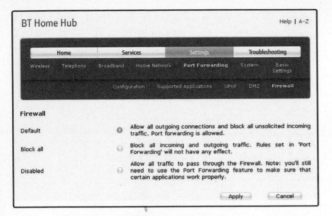

Above: Most routers have in-built firewalls.

Administrator Password

When you first install your router, you will be given an administrator username and password allowing you to access your router settings. It is important to change this as soon as possible to protect your router from being accessed by somebody else. You will normally find the option to do this in the basic settings page or your router configuration.

Router Firewall

You can normally find the settings for your router's firewall under the Port Forwarding or Packet Forwarding settings. You will normally see a number of options for disabling the firewall, blocking all traffic or allowing certain access (usually set as the default).

Firewall Access

As with software firewalls, the firewall on your router may block innocent applications and devices. Because of this, you may need to add exceptions to your firewall.

1. Go into your Port Forwarding settings and look for a menu option that says 'exceptions' or 'configuration'.

2. You may have a menu of listed games and applications that you can simply select to allow access.

Left: Adding an exception to the firewall.

3. If your game or application is not listed, you will have to add it, which means finding out the port range and protocol of the application (see the manufacturer's instructions).

Granting Device Access

Not only can you grant certain access to games and applications, but you can also set up a list of approved devices that can access your router. Sometimes this is described as an access blocking policy, or it may just be listed as access restrictions. If you have a list, you must remember that any new devices you want to connect to the router will have to be added to gain access to the Internet.

Hot TIp

If you have a games console, it is sometimes better to add the device as an exception using Port Forwarding configuration rather than the individual games, as attacks against consoles tend to be quite rare.

ENCRYPTION KEYS AND IDENTIFIERS

Perhaps the most important form of security on a modern wireless router is the encryption key you enter when connecting to the router. Most manufacturers provide each router with a unique key, but is often a good idea to regularly change it.

Hot Tip

Change your SSID in your router setting from the manufacturer's default, as this will prevent hackers from knowing what type of router you have, making it harder for them to hack into it.

SSID

Service Set Identifier (SSID) is the name given to your router that you see in your network settings on your computer or smartphone. By itself, the SSID cannot be used to gain access to your network, but it does let people know your wireless router exists.

SSID Broadcast

Most routers let you prevent your SSID from being broadcast. If you turn this off, devices will not be able to find your router, but those already connected to it will remain connected.

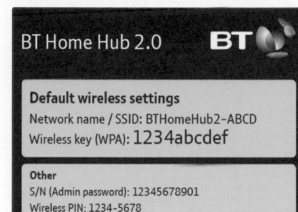

Above: You can usually find all your router details on a sticker on the back.

Encryption Types

Wireless routers come with some form of encryption, which scrambles the data sent over the network. Generally, there are two types of encryption offered by router manufacturers.

○ **WPA (Wi-Fi Protected Access):** A newer, more secure form of encryption. Always opt for this in your router settings if available.

○ **WEP (Wireless Equivalent Privacy):** An older, less secure form of encryption, although it is more compatible with devices than WPA.

Router Position

Finally, where you place your router in your home can affect security. Wireless routers are broadcast devices, so they can reach far beyond the confines of your home. To limit the range, try to install a router as close to the centre of your home as possible, rather than by windows or doors, where the signal can leak out. (This will also give you the best signal.)

JARGON BUSTER

The world of Internet security is full of its own terms and terminology that you may find confusing, so to help you, here is the most common jargon explained.

Adware

Malware designed to display unwanted advertisements. Adware can infect Internet browsers and prevent normal browsing by redirecting you to advertising websites or bombarding you with pop-ups (see also malware).

Antivirus software

Software designed to prevent malware, including viruses, computer worms and Trojans, from infecting computers. Antivirus software can also remove malware and stop spyware and adware threats.

Backdoor

A method used by hackers to bypass normal security procedures on a computer, often caused by vulnerabilities in the software or network.

Bluetooth

A short-range, wireless communication system often used to connect devices such as headphones, smartphones and keyboards.

Bot or web bot

An automated program that performs a set of actions; a bot can be legitimate, such as those used by search engines to crawl websites, or they can be malicious and take control of computers. (See also **Botnet**.)

Botnet

A collection of computers infected with malicious bots that work together to carry out a single act, such as attacking a computer network or spreading malware. Botnets often operate unbeknown to the computer users. (See also **Zombie computer**.)

Cache

Files stored on an Internet browser, such as images and text, that are used to speed up the loading of websites.

Cloud (computing)

Computing services that operate on the Internet, such as applications that can be run without needing to download a program, or storage services that store your files online.

Cookie

A small file stored on your computer by websites, which contains certain details about your web history so a website can remember your log-in details and personal preferences.

Computer virus

A type of malware that infects a computer and can self-replicate and spread to other machines. The term is often used as a catch-all word to describe malware. (See also **Malware**.)

Cracker

A malicious or criminal hacker. (See also **Hacker**.)

Distributed Denial of Service (DoS) attack

Where a number of machines all attack a network at the same time, overloading it and making normal access impossible.

Domain Name System (DNS)

Converts the IP address of a server into an easily recognizable web address that you can type into an address bar.

Digital certificate

Also called public key certificate or security certificate, a digital certificate validates a website by the use of encrypted or digitally signed data.

Domain (address)

The main part of a website name, such as www.google.com. Other web pages on a site can be attached to a domain address by means of a backslash, such as www.google.com/help.

Encryption

A method of scrambling information to make it unreadable to unauthorized users.

Firewall

A hardware or software device that blocks access into a network. Can be used to prevent hackers and malicious software from gaining access.

Hacker

A person who gains unauthorized access to a computer or network, either for malicious purposes or to test security.

Heuristics

Often used to describe a type of antivirus solution that can spot malware by suspicious behaviour rather than having to identify its signature on a database.

HTML

HyperText Mark-up Language is used by websites to design and format web pages.

HTTP

HyperText Transfer Protocol is a set of communication rules for controlling how information is sent over the Internet.

HTTPS

HyperText Transfer Protocol Secure is an encrypted and more secure form of HTTP.

Hyperlink (also just 'link')

An active element such as a word or phrase on a web page that takes you to another destination when you click on it.

Internet

A network of computers and computer networks. Often used interchangeably, although incorrectly, with the World Wide Web, which are the websites that exist on the Internet.

IP address

An Internet Protocol address is a unique numerical identifier for each computer, network or server.

Keylogger

A type of malware or spyware that tracks your keystrokes on a keyboard and sends the data to a third party. (See also **Malware**.)

Laptop

A portable computer.

Malware

Means **mal**icious soft**ware** and describes all types of software designed to cause harm on a computer, including computer viruses, spyware, keyloggers, worms, adware and Trojans.

Network
A group of computers or devices connected together either wirelessly or by cables.

PDA
A Personal Digital Assistant is a type of small computer that can be used to store information such as addresses and telephone numbers, as well as connect to the Internet.

Pharming
An attempt by a hacker to redirect a website's traffic to another site for the purpose of stealing information.

Phishing
An attempt by a hacker or fraudster to obtain personal information about a user, often by posing as someone else or a legitimate company. Phishing is normally done using email, text or social media messages.

Plug-in
An additional component to a software program that adds a new feature or added functionality.

Pop-up
A new browser window, often containing an advertisement, that pops up uninvited in front of an existing page.

Proxy (server)
A computer server that acts as an intermediary between your computer (the client) and the server you are communicating with (the host).

Ransomware
A type of malware that forces you to pay money to unlock files or regain access to your computer.

Registry
A database on Windows machines that stores start-up and configuration settings.

Rootkit
A type of malware designed to hide the fact that a computer has been compromised by hiding itself in the system files or 'root' of a computer. (See also **Malware**.)

Router
A hardware device that connects a computer or network to the Internet either wirelessly or by the use of cables.

Security holes
A weakness in a security system that can be exploited by hackers or malicious software. (See also **Backdoor**.)

Smartphone
A mobile phone that also has many functions of a computer, such as being able to access the Internet.

Spam
Unsolicited emails or messages often containing adverts. Spam can also include phishing messages. (See also **Phishing**.)

Spyware
A type of malware designed to spy on your computer use and collect information about you without your knowledge or permission. (See also **Malware**.)

Tablet computer
A flat touch-screen device that runs similar computing architecture to a smartphone but is usually larger.

Trojan (or Trojan horse)
A type of malware that gains access to a computer by posing as an innocent file or program. (See also **Malware**.)

URL
Uniform Resource Locator is a website's address.

URL spoofing
An attempt by hackers to create a fake website that has a very similar URL to the site it is trying to replicate in order to fool people. Often used in phishing attacks. (See also **Phishing**.)

Virus
See **Computer virus**.

VoIP
Voice over Internet Protocol is a method of voice communication over the Internet.

Web browser
Software designed to connect with and read web pages.

Web page
A page on the Internet generated by HTML that contains information that can be viewed on a web browser.

Website
A collection of web pages under a single domain address.

Web server
A computer that makes web pages and other resources available for sharing over the Internet.

WEP
Wired Equivalent Privacy is type of encryption used by wireless routers.

Wi-Fi
Wireless Fidelity is a short-range wireless technology that enables wireless Internet and network access.

Wi-Fi hotspot
Usually a public wireless access point. Sometimes these locations have poor or no security measures in place.

World Wide Web
The name given to the websites and web pages that are interconnected on the Internet.

Worms
A type of malware that can self-replicate and spread itself around a network. (See also **Malware**.)

WPA (and WPA2)
Wi-Fi Protected Access is a form of wireless encryption that is more secure than WEP.

Zombie computer
A computer that has a bot or other malicious program running in the background without the knowledge or permission of the user.

FURTHER READING

Abagnale, Frank W., *Stealing Your Life: The ultimate identity theft prevention plan*, Broadway Books, 2008

Bailey, Matthew, *The Complete Guide To Internet Privacy, Anonymity And Security*, A Nerel Publication, 2011

Cambridge, Rodney D., *How NOT To Use Your Smartphone: Avoid hackers stealing your identity via your phone*, CreateSpace Independent Publishing Platform, 2012

Cherry, Denny, *The Basics Of Digital Privacy*, Syngress, 2014

Clare, Andrew, *The Rough Guide To Android Phones And Tablets*, Rough Guides, 2012

Donat, Wolfram, *Internet Security 101: Keeping your stuff safe online*, CyberWolf Publishing, 2012

Edgington, Shawn Marie, *The Parent's Guide to Texting, Facebook, and Social Media: Understanding the benefits and dangers of parenting in a digital world*, Brown Books, 2011

Elenkov, Nikolay, *Android Security Internals: An in-depth guide to Android's security architecture*, No Starch Press, 2014

Garfinkel, Simson & Spafford, Gene, *Web Security, Privacy & Commerce*, O'Reilly Media, 2001

Hastings, Glenn & Marcus, Richard, *Identity Theft, Inc.*, Disinformation Company Ltd, 2006

Hruska, Jan, *Computer Viruses And Anti-virus Warfare*, Ellis Horwood Ltd, 1992

Hunter, Nick, *Internet Safety (Hot Topics)*, Raintree, 2011

Ioannou, Nick, *Internet Security Fundamentals: Practical steps to increase your online security*, Boolean Logical Ltd, 2014

Kandasamy, Vijey Ashok, *Anti-virus Implementation For Beginners: A simple guide to implement an anti-virus program*, VDM Verlag Dr. Müller, 2011

LaVine, Howard, *How To Increase Online Security With Smartphones, Tablets and Computers*, 2014

Liu, Ashok, *Computercare's Laptop Repair Workbook: The 300 cases of classic notebook computers troubleshooting and repair*, AuthorHouse, 2012

Lockhart, Andrew, *Network Security Hacks*, O'Reilly Media, 2006

Montgomery, Jim, *Internet Security: Security and privacy on laptops, smartphones and tablets*, CreateSpace Independent Publishing Platform, 2014

Owen, Madison, *How To Protect Your Children Online: Internet safety tips for kids*, CreateSpace Independent Publishing Platform, 2012

Simmons, R.J., *No Trace Left: Internet privacy tips and strategies to protect your personal and financial information*, Sparrow Publications, 2014

Sullivan, Bryan, *Web Application Security, A Beginner's Guide*, McGraw-Hill Osborne, 2012

USEFUL WEBSITES

www.publicproxyservers.com
Find a proxy to browse the Internet anonymously.

www.kproxy.com
Claims to be the most reliable and fastest free anonymous web proxy on the Internet.

https://www.google.com/safebrowsing/report_badware/
Report a site containing malicious software to Google.

https://www.iwf.org.uk/report
Report inappropriate material to the Internet Watch Foundation.

www.uk.safesearchkids.com
Powered by Google, this search engine lets your children browse the web with safe search permanently on.

www.antivirusforum.net/forum.php
Compare and choose between different antivirus software.

www.avg.com
Download the most popular free antivirus software.

www.zonealarm.com
Download a free firewall and find compatible antivirus and security software.

www.adobe.com
Get free trials of Adobe software and free updates for basic plug-ins.

www.malwarebytes.org
For a free downloadable version of anti-malware software.

www.preyproject.com
Download an app that lets you keep track of your laptop, smartphone or tablet whenever missing.

www.cyberghostvpn.com
Set up your own private network when using Wi-Fi hotspots.

www.piriform.com/recuva
Download Recuva, a free Windows program that lets you restore deleted files.

www.piriform.com/ccleaner
Download CCleaner, the free registry-cleaning program for Windows to fix invalid or corrupted entries.

INDEX